Man Magnet:
How to Be the Best Woman You Can Be in Order to Get the Best Man

Also by Romy Miller:

Understanding Women: The Definitive Guide to Meeting, Dating and Dumping, if Necessary

Man Magnet:
How to Be the Best Woman You Can Be in Order to Get the Best Man

By

Romy Miller

the book factory

Man Magnet:
How to Be the Best Woman You Can Be in Order to Get the Best
Man
by
Romy Miller

The Book Factory
an imprint of New Tradition Books
ISBN 1932420452

For information contact:
The Book Factory
newtraditionbooks@yahoo.com

Disclaimer: This book is not intended to replace medical advice or be a substitute for a psychologist. The author and publisher expressly disclaim responsibility for any adverse affects of this book. Neither author nor publisher is liable for information contained herein.

For the man magnets—past, present and future.

Contents

Introduction: What this book is about.

Most women, generally speaking, don't have much trouble attracting men. It's true. You know it and I know it. However, this is not the problem. The problem is that we have trouble attracting the more desirable guys, the good ones. We're all man magnets, even if we're not attracting the "right" guys. I know plenty of women who are bum magnets and lots more who are pest magnets. But there is a special breed of woman who attracts just about any guy she wants. She is a man magnet.

You want to be that woman, don't you? You want to be able to attract the good guys and take your pick. The great thing is, you *can* be that woman. The better thing is, it doesn't take that much to be her. Yes, it will take some work and it will take some time, but you can do it. You've been given everything you need to be able to attract the kind of guy you've always wanted. But first, there's some work that needs to be done.

That's what this book is about. It's about knowing that there is a good guy—or guys—out there for you. Now don't think I am going to tell you it's going to be easy, because it's not. But that doesn't mean you have to make it more difficult than it is. And that's the problem with dating nowadays—everyone is making it difficult. Everyone is a game-player or everyone is looking for someone "perfect" for them. Everyone is making something so innately human into a game that only a fool would play.

That's what we're going to concentrate on. This book is about how to stop playing games with others—and with yourself—and get out there and find a good man. A man who will be nice to you. A man who will love you for you, not for some image you've presented to him in hopes that he'll like you more and want to "keep you around". A man who, simply, loves you. This book can help you do that if you take the initiative to help yourself.

So what makes this book so different from the million or so other dating books out there? This one is honest, that's what. This one is going to be one hard truth after another. I am not going to hold any punches. I'm going to tell you how to be a man magnet, what to look out for and who to avoid. I'm going to dispel myths and, hopefully, some of your frustrations.

On the other hand, if you're perfectly content being single, then this isn't the book for you. Then again, if you were perfectly content being single, you wouldn't have picked it up. This is a no frills kind of book. And sometimes that's the only way we can see things for the way they truly are. It might sting a little at first, but in the end, we're better off knowing the truth.

I'm going to go into detail about how you can turn yourself into a man magnet and attract the best possible guy for you. There are some universal truths and very common sense things that routinely seem to get overlooked. This is the kind of stuff I'm gong to focus on. I'm going to concentrate on teaching you to use what God gave you to land a good man. And about how you can attract men no matter what their social standing is, no matter how good looking they are.

The most important thing this book will teach you is that there's nothing wrong with you. You're not a horrible, unlovable person just because you haven't found someone yet or can't seem to attract the guys you'd really rather be with. It's not your fault. Perhaps you've just been misguided. What's wrong, maybe, is the way you approach dating. If and when you can approach it from a realistic point of view and know what you're up against, then you can truly turn yourself into a man magnet. And once you do that, there'll be no stopping you.

You're a smart girl, aren't you? You're successful and mostly nice to everyone you meet. It's just the guys are so... Well, they're assholes, aren't they? No matter how many men you meet, none of them live up to your expectations or, perhaps, you don't live up to *theirs*. It's all become a hassle, something that you don't look forward to doing. But all that's about to change. Soon, you'll wonder why you thought it was a hassle in the first place.

Keep in mind that this book isn't offering you instant gratification. It's offering you a wake-up call. I will sometimes be harsh but always realistic. I'm not going to tell you how to play games or give you advice that won't work. I am going to tell you how it's done. You deserve the best, right? In order to get it, you have to face reality. I'm going to tell you what works—there's no tricks involved.

The dating/mating game.

Someone once said hope is the mother of all fools. Hope might turn us into fools but that doesn't keep us from doing it, does it? It doesn't keep us from dreaming about a fantasy guy who's going to swoop in and take away all of our problems. Hope is good. It keeps us from not giving up on love, marriage and babies. Hope might be the mother of all fools, but it also enables us to continue on when things look a little bleak. It gives us the desire to fulfill our genetic destiny. And, of course, our genetic destiny is procreation. Without hope, most of us would have given up on getting a good man a long time ago and without a man, procreation can be a tricky business.

It's hard, though, isn't it? It's so hard to keep trying, to hope against hope that someone will materialize and be "The One". It's hard to go to the clubs and survey the room and get that queasy feeling in the pit of our stomachs. It's hard to keep putting ourselves out there with no real tangible results.

But we do, don't we? And we do it because the dating/mating game is one we're genetically engineered to play. Actually we have no choice but to play it and we will play it until we are old and gray. And even when we're old and gray, we will play it if given the choice. Besides that, it's so fun. There's nothing like new love, is there? There's nothing like that nervous little feeling a girl gets when a handsome man zones in on her. There's nothing like receiving that first kiss or having sex with a guy for the first time. Nothing, nothing, nothing. And there's nothing like it because we've been programmed to want and desire it even when it becomes difficult. We can never give up on love because it's not *in* us to give up. Think of our ancestors. If they'd given up, we wouldn't be here now, would we? In essence, if we give up on love, we give up on our very selves.

While all this is well and good, that doesn't take away the fact that men can be very elusive—and that's putting it nicely. At least the ones we want. Sure, we all have a pest or two hanging around who want us like we want rock stars. This makes us want to give up on it all. Where *are* all the good men? And why *do* we care so much? Why do we even *try*?

The reason we try, as I've said, is because it's our genetic destiny. Besides that, it's all biological. If we didn't have it in us to meet and mate, our species would die out. If all of us gave up on love, there wouldn't be any future generations to play the game of love.

Sure, that's a little heavy but it's the truth. We continue this mating game because we really have no choice. It's ingrained in us to get out there and find someone to mate with. It's a drive we've been given without being given the rules for it.

But this is not entirely true. While we haven't been given the rules, we have been given the instinct to know what to do. We just don't listen to it. The key is to listen to our instinct and make it into the rules. If you look at it like this, the rules, in and of themselves are actually pretty darn simple. You grow up, you meet someone, you get married and you have a few babies. That is, if you want to have a few babies. It's all instinctual.

However, the problems arise because now we have "choices". We can prolong marriage and babies indefinitely. We can focus on our careers in lieu of focusing on getting a man. Men aren't our common goal anymore. They're more the icing on the proverbial cake. While this is good in theory, it makes it harder on us when we decide we do want what we've been genetically programmed to want. We don't know how to get it because, due to our "choices", the basic rules aren't so basic anymore.

So the problem lies in the fact that the rules of dating/mating have been "re-worked", and not to our advantage. In fact, the rules have been so skewed over these past few generations that all of us are chasing our tails, wondering why it's so hard and what we're doing wrong. Newsflash: We're not doing anything wrong! We've just been told that these simple rules are wrong and that if we tweak them a little here and there, we can do it better. We've been told this and we've been told that to the point of emotional paralysis. Sometimes, it's just easier to sit home on a Saturday night eating a pint of ice cream instead of getting out there and trying to play the dating game. It gets tiring. It gets old. Why bother with it at all?

But you know why you bother with it and so do I. You bother with it because you can't help *but* bother with it. And it's not anything that you're doing wrong. It's probably something to do with what you've been taught. Everyone wants to give everyone else dating advice, don't they? But too much of anything, especially dating advice, is a bad thing.

Dating advice, really, isn't going to do you much good. And that's because what works for one person will never, ever work for another—there is always exceptions to every rule. Also, the people giving the advice don't know much more than you do. In fact, many of them seem to have gone through one dysfunctional relationship after another just to write a book on dating or give "advice" on it. They're telling you what worked, or rather what hasn't worked, for them or their friends. They're not telling you what's going to work for you. They're also telling you have to date just for the point of dating, not how to actually date with the purpose of starting a relationship. And, worse, they always want you to try to be someone you're not. That is the main problem with these books and with dating.

We all want to be someone special, someone all men will look at and go ga-ga for. The thing is, we're already pretty darn special and we don't have to take on different personas in order to attract a mate. We don't have to do much of anything other than <u>putting ourselves out there as approachable and loveable</u>. Once you do that, the rest is cake.

I am here to tell you I know what works and it's pretty simple when you get right down to it. And what works? <u>Being yourself—b</u>eing who you are, who you were born—is what works. Sure, it's a cliché but clichés exist for a reason.

We're going to go into more detail on that a little later on but what the point I want to get across right now is that dating/mating does not have to be as hard as we've all made it. It doesn't mean you have to spill a million tears before you find a guy to settle down with. It means you can have some fun before you settle down. It means you can find someone special if you so desire. And isn't it time?

In a nutshell:
- The dating/mating game isn't that hard to figure out.
- Stop trying to be something you're not. Be yourself; that's all you need in order to succeed.
- Don't take advice from people who obviously don't know what they're talking about.

The secret to being a man magnet.

First of all, what is a man magnet? A man magnet is a chick who always gets the man she wants. She may or may not be drop-dead gorgeous. She may or may not have the perfect body. But, for some reason, she's always dating and she always has men flock to her. Men *love* this chick. They can't get enough of her. And she has her pick of the flock. There's something very special about this woman.

A man magnet is a woman who is confident, funny and always takes care of herself. She doesn't sit around and wait for a guy to call but she never has to call a guy herself. If a guy she likes starts playing games, she dumps him and moves on. She is a woman who is in control of her own destiny and she doesn't take second best. One day, she will marry and one day she'll probably have kids. But right now, she's having the time of her life.

Man magnets know how to attract men. They just have this innate quality. But you too can acquire this skill. In time, you can hone it and have your pick of any man you desire. I'm here to tell you what a man magnet has and it's not that hard to attain. In fact, all women have it in them already.

So what's she got? What is this quality she has at her disposal that makes men fall for her? I mean, she's not *that* pretty or *that* sweet, is she? No. In fact, she's kind of a bitch. But what is it? What makes her *so* special? Are you ready?

The secret to being a being a man magnet is: Act like a woman.

Feminists everywhere are going to eat me alive over that but so what? It's the cold, hard truth. Men like women who *act* like women. A man magnet knows this. She knows she's a woman and she's not afraid to be one. *That's* her special quality. That's what she does that drives men crazy. She knows she's got something they want and she's not afraid to flaunt it.

Think Scarlett O'Hara before the war broke out. Watch *Gone with the Wind* and you'll get what I'm saying.

Sure, women have fought to get to the point where we're equal to men and all that, but, really, if we all end up alone, what good did it do us? What good is equality if we can't have what's naturally ingrained in us to want? We all want that big, strong man. And all men want a woman. All straight men, that is.

The good news is that you don't have to develop this—it's already there, inside of you. All you have to do is bring it out. God gave you everything you need in order to attract the opposite sex. You have the power within to get the man you want. It's just lying there, dormant. All you have to do is wake it up. This starts by you adjusting your attitude.

Does this mean you can get any man out there? Well, no, because some men are married or live in different countries and, besides that, there are always extenuating circumstances. We're talking about men who are somewhere in your world, as in living in your town. We're talking about *available* men.

You lament, "But they don't seem to want me!" And, "It seems as though they all want the same type of woman who is beautiful and built like a brick shithouse."

It doesn't matter.

This book is about getting a man so you can start that life you've always wanted, which may or may not include a white picket fence. And it all starts by you waking up and realizing you already have what you need in order to attract a mate.

But first of all, let's get a few things out of the way.

In a nutshell:

- A man magnet is a woman who *acts* like a woman.
- A man magnet isn't afraid of her female qualities and uses them to her benefit.

Ms. Independent.

There are several types of women out there who seem unable to get or keep a man. I believe this is because they've got issues going on *outside* of dating. The next few chapters are going to concentrate on these women. You may or may not see yourself in these chapters, but if you do, don't get pissed off. Just read and let it sink in. Remember, I told you this wasn't going to be easy. But, again, you don't have to make it hard. If you face up to these issues, you're going to be able to do this great thing called "letting it go". And the only way to get over something is to face up to it. Without first doing that, you can't ever hope to overcome obstacles in your path.

Let's get talk about Ms. Independent first.

Ms. Independent. You know who you are. You never get close to any man, or anyone else for that matter besides your few, trusted friends and family. You don't get close because you don't want anyone to interfere with your life. You don't need any help and not only can you do anything, you can always do it better.

If I've seen it once, I've seen it a thousand times. You meet this really great guy. Sure, you could find fault with him if you looked hard enough, but, hey, who's looking? Certainly not you, at least not right now. You've been on a million dates and are still looking for "The One". And this could be him! You and said date go out and you have a great time. At the end of the date, he gives you a peck on the cheek and then... Then he doesn't call. You spend God only knows how much lamenting on whether you wore too much perfume or were too talkative or whatever. You fixate on it until you drive yourself absolutely crazy. But the fact still remains that he didn't call, did he? Maybe you went on a second date or a third date but now he's pulling away and doesn't seem to be that interested anymore. What went wrong?

I'd be willing to bet that you're an independent, self-sufficient woman who doesn't "need" a man in her life. But you certainly "want" a man, or three. You know, for companionship and stuff. And you would like to get laid sometime this decade, right? Your eggs are wailing inside you, *It's time!* It's time to find that man and get on with it. But what went wrong with the date? And why does this always seem to happen?

Plain and simple, you scared him off. You are tough and career-driven. You are attractive, you dress well and you smell nice. Your home makes his place look like a dump and that expensive watch on your wrist tells him everything he needs to know: You can take care of yourself. Fact is, if you can take care of yourself so well, why do you need him at all?

There's nothing wrong with being career-driven and focused. However, some men see this as off-putting. They want to be in control as it's in their chemical make-up to be the aggressive one. If they weren't, then none of us would have survived our caveman days. If they hadn't aggressively stalked and killed animals for us to eat, we wouldn't be talking about all this stuff now.

But we don't need them like we used to, do we? Men are great, but are they worth the trouble? Are they worth the money we spend on clothes and pedicures? We can order in if we get hungry and, if worse comes to worse, we can go to a sperm bank for a baby.

Pretty depressing, if you ask me.

The problem is that you spend all day being ambitious and you can't turn it off once you meet a man. Your relationship turns into a competition. So controlling you are. You have to prove you can do anything he can. Let's face it, lady, you can't. You can't fertilize your own eggs and you can't lift a fifty pound box over your head. Be a woman and let him be the man. That's all he wants. Let him know how big and strong he is. But most importantly, you are going to have to learn to leave your career at work. Career and ambitious women do get the job done, but once you've punched the clock, turn it off.

But how do you turn it off? One way is just to forget about it. Don't lie awake at night staring at the ceiling worrying about your job as it is not the sum total of who you are. Learn to separate yourself from your career. When you're at work, work, but when you're not, don't. When you go on a date, don't try to impress him with all your accomplishments. Sit back and enjoy what's happening in the moment before you start planning your future together. After your relationship is established, then you can begin to share.

No, this doesn't mean to be someone other than who you are. This means to learn to turn it off, or at least down a little. Sure, you should be proud of your accomplishments, but you have to find a way to be approachable and vulnerable because if you give off a vibe that you don't need a man, he'll get the point. I'm not saying to fall over him with the whole "damsel in distress" scenario, but he needs to know he's needed. He needs to know he contributes something. Besides that, men are very competitive and if they date a woman who's more successful than they are, they're going to feel as though they don't measure up.

It's a hard truth, but men like to compete *with other men*. Women, not so much. It's that whole fragile male ego thing. He doesn't want to feel belittled or like he can't take care of you if you need him to. If he feels this, he's going to hit the door. He's got enough issues of his own without having a woman make him feel insignificant.

But what's the big deal? Why don't men want to be with independent, successful women? Because they scare the living daylights out of them. Well, not really. It's because they think they have nothing to offer you. If you've got it all and you've got it under control, then what can they offer you? And, again, they don't want to compete with you. They want to be in charge—or at least think they are. If you've already got everything taken care of, there's not much room for that, is there?

The independent woman intimidates guys. If you can fix your own car and carry your own bags and repair the radiator, what good is he going to be to you? Sure, sometimes, you will make more money than some of the guys you run across and that's okay. But you need to know this makes guys feel inferior. So when this happens, he needs to make it up in some other way, such as repairing your car or something like that. If he can't do *something*, he's going to feel emasculated. No man wants to feel inferior to a woman. Hard fact of life, but it's true.

However, don't think this necessarily means men want to feel superior to you because they don't. They want someone they can work with. They want to be able to offer something to the relationship. They want someone they can help out sometimes by doing manly things like changing the oil in your car or squashing a bug. They want you to be a woman. They have to know they're physically stronger than you and can protect you if anything happens. If you can take care of yourself, that's great. But you have to know, he wants to take care of you, too.

Also, men want someone they can grow with, that can teach them how to be more sensitive. They want you to be nonjudgmental and Ms. Independent always gives off that judgment vibe. "What kind of loser she must think I am. I don't make as much money as her. What could I possibly offer her?"

He can offer you his love that's what.

When you're out with a guy, let him be the man. Of course, as I've said, don't go all "damsel in distress" on him, but allow him to treat you like a woman, like a lady. Allow him to carry your bags or pull your chair out for you. Allow him to be masculine. Remember he's always the big, strong man. Even if he's just cooking dinner for you, he's strong. Lean over, touch his bicep and say, "Ohhh, nice." Let him know that you like the fact that he's bigger and stronger than you. This gives him confidence. It strokes his fragile male ego like nothing else. It also makes him think amorously of you. "She's thinks I'm strong. She likes me. I like her, too." (Keep in mind that most men will acknowledge a woman's strengths if *she* will acknowledge *his*.)

More importantly, men need to know that they can protect you, that they can shelter you. If you've got everything taken care of, he'll think there's no room in your life for a bozo like him.

It's as simple as that. Men, truthfully, aren't that hard to figure out. They all pretty much want the same thing. Sure, some of them are self-serving louses but as you go along, you'll know how and when to weed those guys out. You don't want a louse. You want a man who wants to be there for you, who wants to help you and make you feel better if you had a bad day.

Sure, in a way, you're playing games, but that's what he wants. All you're doing is breaking it down to the primal level. If he's got you all figured out from the get-go, there's nothing for him to latch onto. Men love a challenge. It makes them feel all manly.

Also, this is what we're all set up for. You've just got to learn how to use it to the best of your advantage. And don't hesitate, either. This is how it really works.

In a nutshell:

- Try to find a way to turn off your job once you've punched the clock.
- Men don't like to compete with women. Sorry, but it's true.
- Men want someone they can grow with, someone they feel they can protect. If he feels like you don't need him for anything, he's not going to need you.
- Don't make him feel inferior to you.

I'm not settling!

Now let's talk about Ms. I-Want-A-Rich/Attractive Man. This is also known as the "I'm not settling!" syndrome.

This type of woman finds fault with every man she's ever dated. He's too this or not enough of that and blah, blah, blah. She wants her man to be perfect and if he's not, she's not going to settle. As a result of this kind of thinking, she's in a cycle of loving them and leaving them. But right about now, she's getting tired of it mainly because most of the men she dates treat her like crap. And if not, she treats them like crap and dumps them.

Is this you?

If you have an attitude of, *"But I want someone perfect for me and I won't settle for less"*, then you might want to prepare to spend your life alone. This is just a way for you to tell yourself that you'd rather be alone than put yourself out there. I mean, have you ever taken into consideration that it might be you who has the problem?

Don't start crying yet.

Yes, we know that you're looking for the ideal man. Let's all take a moment, close our eyes and envision him. He's got everything you want and need: *Man, he looks so good!* Or you could have found the ideal man in a book you read: *I want one just like that!* You see him in the movies: *Man he would make a great dad!* Problem is, these dudes aren't real and the actors who play them are usually:

- Gay.
- On drugs.
- Womanizers.
- Premature ejaculators.

Another thing, the fantasy guy you saw on TV doesn't even exist. He's created just to get you to buy stuff! He's there so you will spend your money on new shampoo and movies and throat lozenges or whatever is being sold at the time. He's the ideal man and is *the figment of someone's imagination.*

It's like this: You've developed this perfect fantasy of the prefect man and the perfect life. You want it and damn it, you won't settle for less. Nothing is going to stop you from getting the man you want, who, by the way, you've never met or even seen on the street.

Reality check: You could meet Mr. Perfect but the first time he does something wrong, you will have to go back to fantasy land. Everyone has fantasies but when these fantasies keep you from living, they're no longer harmless. And if you have a fantasy of Mr. Perfect then you're cheating yourself out of a lot of good living and enjoyment. It's okay to go off into fantasy land from time to time, it's just not okay to *live* in fantasy land. If you're living like this, you need to pull yourself together before you become too fixated on it so that no guy will ever measure up. Hopefully you'll do this before it's too late.

If you're saving yourself for the "perfect" guy, ask yourself this: What if he never comes along? What if you never meet him? You might not, you know. No one is perfect. Not you, not me, not that hunky gym instructor. Get this: No one will ever be perfect. Get over it and get on with your life.

Did you know that the use of "perfect" as a verb is "to finish"? Look it up. It means he's done. And when you meet him, if he's perfect, there ain't much you can do with him.

I once read a tidbit in a magazine about a very handsome and famous so-called perfect man who had dandruff so bad that it would coat the collars of his expensive suits. One day he was out with his equally famous girlfriend who became very pissed off at him because of it. So you see, even if you do get a guy like that, he's still going to have a fault or two. And that's because men are human. Just like you, they've all got a little something that isn't perfect.

Of course, we have been genetically programmed to want the best man possible to father our children. This is not news. All women want a strong man and there's nothing wrong with that. But sometimes it goes too far and we forget that while men can be strong, they can't be prefect. Unfortunately, perfect men are in short supply. I don't think there's anything wrong with trying to find one, and, if you can, good for you. If you can't, why not take a look at a regular Joe who actually exists in this reality?

This isn't about lowering your standards. This is about opening your eyes and seeing men for who they truly are. It's about taking matters into your own hands and doing something about your situation. If you go in with an attitude that you're "settling" then you are missing the point. And the point is to find someone you can care about who will care about you. Remember, after you're done, he's still going to be *him*. You can't—and shouldn't want to—change his personality.

Now the good news. If you're still reading, you're probably over fantasy guy. In fact, if you ever do see him, you'll kick his ass. You're ready to settle down with a regular Joe and get on with the business of life. Good for you.

But keep in mind that, in the end, the regular Joe is still a man and will do things to piss you off like leave socks on the floor from time to time. You need to realize that no matter what, if you look hard enough, you can always find something wrong with him. We're all human and we all have faults, even you. Learning to accept that is the number one thing you can do to gain a fulfilling relationship. Try not to look so hard for fault. Once you can start doing that, you can be more forgiving of normal human characteristics.

After all this you still might say to yourself, "I'd rather be alone!" Well, that's fine. Say hello to your cats for me.

In a nutshell:

- "Not settling" is just another way to tell yourself you prefer to be alone.
- There are no perfect guys. They're just men.
- See if you can get your fantasy guy and if not, why not give a regular Joe a chance?
- If you look for fault, you will find it. Try not to look so hard and learn to be more forgiving of human attributes.

The Single Girl Syndrome...

...will only *keep* you single. If I've heard it once, I've heard it a gazillion times: "There are no good men out there!" Wah wah wah.

You're not getting any younger and you do want to get married and have a kid or two someday, don't you? But, damn it, where are all the good men? Well, I'll tell you where they are. They're everywhere! Just take a look around. No, I mean it. *Take a look around.* See? There's one right now. And over there... Wow. There are a lot of men around. But...but...

But something is stopping you. It might be the fact that you're somewhat insecure or, perhaps, you're too busy living it up in the big city, being the single girl. Maybe you're too caught up having a good time with your girlfriends and your gay male friends to even think about settling down. You've spent a fortune on clothes and beauty treatments. You've starved yourself and for what? To end up by yourself after everyone else has gotten married?

Sure, maybe you've been dumped and put upon and all that other crap. You can blame it all on the men if you so desire, but more than likely it's not the men who have done it to you, it's you who has done it to yourself. You have kept yourself from finding a guy to love and marry by all these silly little notions you thought up in the second grade. You've kept yourself emotionally distant as you live in a dream world, wondering when your prince charming will come and find you. You're living a life similar to one you read a million times in one of those single girl books.

It's time for a reality check. You're older now. Face it.

Let's talk about the single girl. Isn't she lovely? She's cute and so loveable. She hops from one man to another without a care in the world. But she's afraid to commit to just one man, or she wants this other man who's unattainable. She goes from one lame-brained situation to another and in the end, she's usually no better off than when she started. In the end, more than likely, this chick is going to end up alone. In the old days, she would have been called an old maid or, worse, a spinster.

Sorry, but the truth hurts. If you want to be that carefree single girl living it up in the big city, then go for it. But know that if you never stop and have a relationship at any time in your life, you can never truly grow as a human being and you can never experience the joy of allowing someone to know the "real you".

And, as we get older, that window of love opportunity slowly closes. Sorry, but it does. If you keep yourself "off the market" for too long, you're going to end up being indefinitely shelved. The majority of us only get a few shots at true, romantic love. Yet, many women overlook their opportunities because the guy is too "this" or not enough of "that". They get so caught up in the single girl lifestyle that they wake up and realize: "Hey, I'm forty—or older—and I've never been married, never been in a 'real' relationship, and I'm alone."

Another thing is that people get too hung up on that initial feeling of attraction and once it dwindles a little, they get scared and bolt. They never seem to understand that when a relationship progresses into maturity, it doesn't get stale, it just evolves. Romantic love does change into attachment love. The single girl knows nothing about this because she never moves from romantic love to attachment.

She can't get attached. If she gets attached, she loses her carefree lifestyle.

It's scary, I know, but as I've said, I told you I wasn't going to pull any punches. This doesn't mean for you to feel bad about yourself. It just means to wake up. You've still got time. I don't want to make this seem like you should be desperate for love or whatever, but I do think one of the major causes of this is that we get hung up on things. And we erroneously think that we don't "need" love. But, in my opinion, we do need love. Love does something to us. It makes us grow in ways we never thought about. It makes us feel like we have a place in the world. Sure, this makes me sound like a hopeless romantic, but I do feel that we are put on earth to mate. Maybe it just makes me sound old-fashioned, but how many of these so-called real single girls have you seen actually look happy? Think about it.

Another problem is that we're so celebrity focused in this day and age that it's skewed our reality. When we read magazines and tabloids about how this celebrity or that celebrity breaks up with one just to go onto another that's equally as gorgeous and rich, we get it into our heads that we can do this too. *But we can't.* We, as normal humans, don't have near the opportunity celebrities do for just simply meeting new people. If we did, there wouldn't be a single girl syndrome.

We were meant to mate. We were meant to have relationships and fall in love. By taking a risk and loving someone, you say to yourself, "I love myself and I am giving myself over to love. I am willing to take that chance."

But what if you end up getting hurt? You end up getting hurt, that's what. There isn't a girl out there who hasn't at some point had her heart broken. Every girl has been susceptible to that at one time or another. Yet, I think it's unhealthy to look at it from the perspective that all love dies and everyone ends up hurt and alone. The great thing about being in a relationship with someone is that, even if you get hurt, you can still learn so much about yourself by taking that chance. And that's what life is really all about—learning and growing. One way to do it is to be in a relationship that will help you become a better person. And if you get hurt, then you move on and you will more than likely move on to a better guy and a better relationship.

However, by stopping the relationship before it can start—for whatever reason—you're doing yourself a great injustice. By being in a relationship, we can learn so many things about ourselves. We can heal past wounds and move on from hurtful times. Being in a relationship with someone who cares about you is the best thing in the world. And not only do they care about you, but you can care about them. By doing this, it allows the love to flow freely and really makes a person content and happy. It's almost like this is what we're supposed to be doing and when we don't, things go crazy.

So, the single girl syndrome is all cute and funny but it's just entertainment; it's not a lifestyle we should aspire to. Ask yourself if this is what you want. Sure, you might get into a relationship and get hurt, but if you never try, then you'll never know. And if you never know, it'll drive you crazy. Why not get all this crap out of your head once and for all and move on with your life? Why not give yourself—and love—a chance? What do you really have to lose but your fear of commitment?

In a nutshell:
- The single girl syndrome will only keep you single.
- If you're perfectly content being single, good for you.
- We were meant to mate.

Love is not a romantic comedy.

And then there's the ideal of Mr. Right. All girls want a Mr. Right. There's also this rumor going around that Mr. Right is just around the corner and he's waiting just for you. He's even got candy and flowers! Just hold on for a little while longer and he will swoop in, sweep you off your feet and give you everything you've ever desired: A big diamond engagement ring, beautiful children, a huge, tastefully decorated home, and many orgasms.

That's right. So just sit back and wait. He'll be here any minute. Hold on. Have some patience! What are a few more hours of your life when you've been waiting for him for years? He's coming! And he is so cute. Your mother is going to love him. Your girlfriends are going to be so jealous they'll turn green. Your dad will even like him and say, "Now I can see her with a guy like that!"

Still waiting? Ask yourself this: *How long have I been waiting for this guy?* If it's been minutes, that's okay. If it's been years, it's not. You're not the only girl in the world who's been sitting around waiting for that bastard, Mr. Right. You're not the only who's been fooled into believing he's out there, either.

Girl, it is time to wake up and smell the coffee.

The time has come for you to do something about meeting that "someone special", hasn't it? It's time because, well, thirty is coming up soon. Or, maybe thirty has come and gone and forty is coming up. And if it's fifty…well you get the point.

Let me tell you something about Mr. Right. He's an urban legend. He's a romantic myth. He's not cool and he's not handsome and that's because he doesn't exist. We want him to exist because, well, we've all had a lot of bad boyfriends and we should get *something* for wasting our time with them.

The problem is that we've all been poisoned by the idea of a perfect life/man which has been perpetuated by Hollywood. Yeah, that's right. Movies make you want something that never existed and can never attain. The even bigger problem is that no matter how bad you want it, no matter how much you "deserve" it, it's not gonna happen.

Listen. So many women buy into these romantic comedies because, well, it seems like a really nice life to have. Women search for this ideal which was a fantasy in someone else's head before they filmed it and made it into "reality". The only thing is that it's not real. It's a bunch of hogwash that makes a person feel horrible about their life because none of us can achieve these heights presented on the screen. We are but mere mortals.

Take any number of "romantic comedy" movies—they are all pretty much the same. In each of these movies we have Mr. Right. Of course, he's attractive and he's brilliant and successful and just damn near perfect. Then you have the Good Girl who is looking for Mr. Right. The Good Girl is beautiful, wears a size zero and is so stylish it hurts. The only thing missing from her life is someone to spend it with. She "finds" Mr. Right by some silly little coincidence and, of course, he's already taken or there's something wrong with him she has to fix. The movie now concentrates on these two bumbling idiots hooking up. We are shown idyllic encounters and romantic dinners and…don't they just look perfect together? Their apartments look so tidy and stylish and nice. They take long bubble baths that look so comforting and relaxing. And in the end, they finally get together and have this fabulous wedding. The Good Girl is dressed in this jaw-dropping dress and Mr. Right is beyond handsome in his tux. The end.

What's wrong with this picture?

Well, for one thing, it's not based in reality. Sure, we want that kind of life because it looks so damn good. *Mr. Right is out there*, we say to ourselves, *if only I wait for him. I can and will have that life I saw in a movie. It can work out like that! He will make everything perfect in my life and he will take me away from all of this and I will live happily ever after.*

The reason we want lives like we see in the movies is because we feel our own lives don't measure up to this ideal. Our lives are boring and uncomplicated. So in order to make ourselves feel better, we decide to wait and see if Mr. Right will turn up. That way, we create a little drama, don't we? Just like they do in the movies and on TV. But the sad reality is you, more than likely, won't get a happy ending.

We have become so brainwashed by the media that a normal guy can't cut it anymore. Get real. Most guys are normal. And so are you. I have seen many women turn up their noses at good men just because they don't look like a movie star or drive an expensive car. Those women are going to end up alone.

Remember, the bigger the car, the bigger the ego.

We're told by the media and the TV to always be young and never settle for second best. The only problem with this is that if we never "settle" then we can never experience the real joy of being with someone who loves and cares about us. To have someone care about you who's not only willing to listen to your problems, but *wants* to, is the best feeling around. It's like finding a pair of designer shoes at a thrift store for fifty cents. No, it's better than that. It really and truly is. Remember, you are not looking for Mr. Right. You are looking for Mr. Right *For You.*

This is why you have to make a conscious decision to get that Hollywood ending crap out of your head. Life is reality. It is not a made up movie about a romantic couple getting together. All you have to do to get over this is to not be afraid of kissing a few frogs when you're hunting the right man. In fact, it's good to kiss a few so when you find the guy you want to keep, you'll appreciate him even more.

On the flip side of this is the dilemma of "settling", which I touched on in the previous chapter. For some reason, we all have it in our heads that if we hook up with Joe Average, we will never get what we "really and truly deserve". What many women want is a man who has all the qualities they dreamt up when they were children and have built up over the years. It usually goes a little something like this: "I'll never be happy if I don't get a man who's rich, famous, has a big penis and a great sense of humor."

You're right. You never will be happy because you're giving yourself an ultimatum. In effect, you're telling yourself you have to get a man with these qualities which are pretty darn hard to come by in everyday life; otherwise you'll just stay single. Even if you found this man, he'd never measure up to your expectations. *You're looking for a guy who doesn't exist.*

Face facts. Men are human. That means they don't have superpowers. That means most weren't born with the ability to live up to unrealistic expectations.

This isn't about some guy living up to your expectations. It's about you facing reality. It's about you coming down from the romantic Hollywood world where all the guys are handsome and make lots of money. It's about you making a conscious choice to give a regular guy a chance. That way, he can give you a chance, too. Believe me, once you find a guy who loves you and that you love, all the money in the world won't make a difference. If you never take a chance, you can never find true love. Again, that might make me sound like a hopeless romantic, but it's true.

This may all sound a little radical but ask yourself: *How long have I been waiting for Mr. Right?* Mr. Right doesn't exist and if he does, who says you are Mrs. Right? Come on! Grow up! If you want to get married someday, some of these silly notions are gonna have to go. If you really and truly want to find a man and get married and do all that good stuff, you can. But you can't sit around and wait for him. He's not just going to miraculously materialize like he does in the movies.

It's time, isn't it? It's time to stop waiting and start taking action. It never rains men and Mr. Right is usually gay. Get over it and find yourself a real man.

Ready? Then let's get to it.

In a nutshell:
- Mr. Right doesn't exist.
- Most guys are just average, everyday kind of people, kind of like you.
- Find yourself a real man who will love your for you. You can do the same for him.
- Be prepared to kiss a few frogs.
- Come down from fantasy land and give a regular guy a chance.
- Realistically speaking, most men have qualities that most women want. He doesn't have to be movie star handsome or rich for you to love him.
- If you never take a chance, you can never find true love.
- Remember that you're not looking for Mr. Right. You're looking for Mr. Right For You.

He's confused.

And with good reason. Women send out so many different signals to men a person would have to be a rocket scientist to interpret them.

Men, bless their hearts, do try to figure us out. They read books and surf the internet in search of that elusive thing that will tell them everything they need to know about chicks. And, ladies, let's face it, all they really need to know is that when it's PMS time, it's time to keep their distance. And, of course, that there is no reason to explain the desire and need for chocolate.

The point is it's time for women to give men a break. It's time to let all that battle of the sexes thing die down for a while. If you think you're confused about men, think about how most men feel about women. They really are confused—not to mention a little scared—and that makes them eager to please us and willing to do anything to get our attention. And that makes them appear desperate, which makes them look pathetic. Which makes us not want anything to do with them.

So, overlook this. Be that woman who is willing to take a chance and give a guy a break. Be that woman who doesn't snub her nose at good/normal guys, the ones who are trying their best to please us.

Perks of being with a "normal" guy:
- He probably has a good job.
- He's probably wants to settle down soon, too.

- He can fix stuff. (You might be able to get him to change the oil in your car and stuff like that.)
- He has a good work ethic.
- He wants the same things as you do and that includes marriage and babies.
- When he falls for you, he will really fall for you. No other woman will matter to him once you've got him hooked.
- He won't stare at himself in the mirror for prolonged periods of time.
- He won't run off when the "going gets tough".
- He'll listen to you and try to help you with your problems.

Be open to any possibility and that means being open to someone who isn't drop dead gorgeous or an internet millionaire. Just be open. Once you can do this, you will begin to invite all kinds of men into your life. Hopefully, most of them will not be creepy and more than a few will be compatible with you.

In a nutshell:
- Men are just as confused about women as women are about men.
- Give the guys a chance.

Grab an eraser.

Today, right now, this minute, grab an eraser and wipe your slate clean. That's right, do it. Erase everything in your past and forget all of your mistakes and bad boyfriends and terrible one night stands. I mean, if you have these things to forget about, of course.

What has happened in your past does not have to taint—or dictate—your future and you shouldn't let it. So what if your last boyfriend dumped you? That doesn't mean you weren't "good" enough. It simply means you weren't compatible and he did you a favor. *Yes, he did.* Even if it still hurts, know that by him breaking up with you, he has saved you a lot of trouble. This means there is someone better for you out there. *Yes, it does.* Having that kind of experience will help you later on. By having it, you will know what to look out for and, possibly, won't repeat past mistakes or bad choices.

Like I was saying, wipe everything off your slate. Imagine doing it. Wipe off all those dating blunders and all those bad relationships. Forget about the guys who "forgot" to call. They weren't worth your time anyway. Unfortunately, they probably had no intention of calling in the first place. These guys aren't good enough to shine your shoes. I say to hell with these guys. Say it with me, ladies: To hell with these guys! Next time you can "forget" to call them.

Erase the guys who used you. Forget about all the embarrassing situations you've been in. And, again, get rid of all the memories of your one night stands. If they make you cringe, just know you weren't using good judgment then but now you've regained your senses and won't do it again. It's in the past and there is no sense in reliving it, i.e. punishing yourself. And, really, that's all you're doing. So stop it.

Now throw out all that you've been taught by the media, your girlfriends and your mother. Wipe away whatever advice that was given to you that wasn't necessarily in your best interest. Get rid of it. Dump it like a bad, stinky boyfriend. Clear your mind of all the mumbo-jumbo.

Get rid of all that Hollywood fairy tale stuff in your head. Wipe it away for good. And wipe away Mr. Right, too. When you're done with that, wipe away the idea of "settling". Remember, you're not going to settle for less, you're going to settle into something that is better for you in the end. Like having someone care about you and remember your birthday.

After you've done that, erase all those things other women have told you about yourself. Like when so and so said you were fat or weren't that smart or whatever. We all know women can be bitches. We all know that other woman can intimidate us and make us feel like crap. Forget those bitches. Don't let them stop you. Chances are, if they put so much effort into making you feel bad about yourself, it's because they feel bad about themselves. Also, you probably have something they are extremely jealous of. It's true. *Yes, it is.* It took me years to figure that out. Don't let it take you years. Erase all those old hags. Let them go bother someone else.

The most important thing you can do after you've wiped your slate clean is to make your own rules to dating. That's right. Decide what you want to do and do it. Make your own rules to getting a man and to keeping one. No one should decide what is best for you but you. Forget everything you've learned or have been taught. Make your own rules by using my guidelines, but shape them into what works best *for you.* Everyone is different and that means what works for one will never work for another.

From now on, you are in control of your destiny. Your past doesn't have to taint you any longer. Make a vow to start a new day today. Once you start with a clean slate, you can start anew. Starting anew will rid you of all your encumbrances and allow you to free up space in your mind for better guys. It will allow you to start fresh. And once you do that, there will be no stopping you.

One last thing, if you have "issues"—broken heart, bankruptcy, etc.—to work on, work on them before you drag someone else into your life. Start a journal, see an accountant or a therapist, anything you have to do to get over this stuff which is holding you back. Once you're free of that, you'll be free to move on to the better things in life which you deserve. So, start afresh, start anew and wipe your slate clean. Bye-bye old, hello new.

In a nutshell:
- Visualize wiping your past experiences away.
- Make your own rules to dating.
- Vow to start anew today.
- If you have "issues", try your best to get over them before finding a new guy.

Catch me if you can.

Women need to realize that wanting to be treated as anything other than a woman, i.e. like "one of the guys" is total stupidity. When we become more aggressive than the man or start acting like a guy by chasing after him, he gets confused. And he runs away.

How to tell if you're too aggressive? You zero in on a guy and stalk him like prey. Or, when you get his attention, you won't let go of it. You use forceful body language and you stare them dead in the eye at all times. When you do this, guys feel as though their power is being drained from them. And, as I've said, it makes them want to run away. Keep in mind that it's *their* job to chase *you*.

Everywhere in the animal kingdom the male has to work to get their female. I recently watched an animal show and was amazed at the lengths other male species go to in order to get their ladies. They were snarling at other males, spitting at them, fighting, getting beaten up, sometimes even killed. They did anything and everything they had to do in order to mate, even if it meant risking their lives. For example, zebras have to fight with the father of their desired female *for days* before dad relents and lets him have his daughter. And the zebra doesn't take any breaks.

You probably think that it's not like that with humans, don't you? Well, it is. If you let him know you're worth the effort, he will fight for you. He'll gladly make a fool out of himself to get you. That's the way he's been genetically programmed. Intelligence really doesn't play into it. Let me rephrase that: For some males, intelligence doesn't play into it. As with anything, there are exceptions to the rule.

There are some human males who are dumb enough to think they can get away without working for a mate. This might be because there are women out there who chase after men. This is always a bad idea if you ask me, but many women do. They find the "perfect" guy and they hunt him down. They do his work for him and the thing is, if they'd just give the guy a chance, he'd probably do *his* job by chasing *them.* But they get impatient and don't want him to "get away". But this is all wrong. If the male doesn't come to you, if he doesn't "track" you down or pay for dinner or any of that, it means he probably doesn't really want you. Sorry. It's harsh, I know. Sure, they might go out with you a few times and they'll always want to sleep with you, but will they commit? Probably not. These guys are not worth your time. They will drain you emotionally and sometimes financially.

On the other hand, you can't make him work *too* hard or he might just come to the conclusion that you're not "worth" it. You can't overdo it. This means being friendly but not guarded. This means having an outgoing personality but not being too aggressive. Remember, he's the aggressor, not you. You are the target. It's up to him to make the move once you've sent the signal.

Again, men want to chase you. They want you to be "unavailable". It's in their genetics and has been carried over from their hunting days. They are the natural born aggressor. It's true. They have to be the aggressor. Watch any *Wild Kingdom* episode and you will find that it is their biological imperative to do so. If you take the lead, his testosterone levels will plummet and you'll scare him off. That's why it's important for you to let him do his job. *Don't do it for him.* He doesn't want you to because it puts him in a subordinate role. If you make the first move and do all the work, he might think you have bigger balls than he does.

So what do you do? *You do what feels right.* Keep in mind that every man is different and that means what works with one man won't work with another. Always listen to your inner voice. It will guide you and it will keep your from making a fool out of yourself. Never get ahead of yourself. If you can stop and learn to listen to your intuition, it will save you a lot of trouble. This is called a hunch. If the hunch is to approach, then he might be shy. So, therefore, approach with caution but always act like you're just passing by. You can just ask him if he has the time.

The funny thing about this is that all you have to do to get 'em interested is to act like you're not interested. And by that I mean, act like you don't want them. Well, more specifically, act like you might be slightly interested but not much. Sure, you think he's okay...but...you might have to wash your hair on Saturday night.

Get what I'm saying? If you do this, it inspires them to chase you. This inspires desire. This makes them think there's something special about you.

And, no, I'm not saying for you to be a super bitch or too aloof. I'm just saying never be too eager when you first meet a guy you like. Give him a little rope, but never enough to make him think you're easy. Guys do not want you to be easy, *ever.* If he is totally unchallenged by you, why should he bother? What's there for him to latch onto?

It's like this. The more interested you act, the more they back away. They feel like they're smothering. It might be something to do with insecurity, I'm not sure. It's probably something to do with their fragile male ego. However, the less interested you act, the more they want you. It's crazy, but it's the truth.

It's a funny game, this game of love, isn't it? But if you know how to play it, it won't take any time for you to land the man of your dreams. And that means acting like a woman and allowing the man to act like a man. This is just the way the game of love is played. Nothing more, nothing less. A woman needs to know a man will work a little to "get" her. This lets her know he'll stick around for the babies, if they happen to come. A man needs to chase because this makes him feel like the "reward"—you—he gets in the end will be worth the trouble. Let him chase. If he doesn't get to chase, it's almost like you've emasculated him. God gave him balls for a reason, girls. Let him use them. It's almost as if you chase him first, he doesn't get to be in charge and the game is being played for him, not *by* him.

Men think if it's too easy, then there must be a catch. They figure there's something "wrong" with a woman who's too "easy". It's a harsh reality but learn to accept it and you'll be home-free. Learn how to give him enough to show you're interested but not enough to make him think he doesn't have to work for it. Do this and you'll be unstoppable.

In a nutshell:
- Men want to chase. They're genetically programmed to do it. Therefore, *let him chase.*

The supermodel principle.

Men don't want women to be "easy". Whether it's getting that date or trying to get them into bed, they just don't like it when we're easy. If we're easy, if we come on too strong, we reek of desperation. Warning bells will go off inside his little head. Never forget that men want to play the game, so let them play the game and do the pursing. You have to concede on this. It doesn't work any other way. And, besides that, if you come on too strong and you "get" him, he'll always wonder why you were so easy.

It's the supermodel principle. Most normal guys know they don't have a chance with a supermodel but they always try, don't they? *Always.* Supermodels make them work—that's one reason they love them so much. Supermodels are "unattainable", therefore, they are the best—in men's minds—and they are worth fighting for, making a fool out of themselves over, being turned down by.

Be a supermodel man magnet. Yes, you can do it.

You lament, "But I'm not pretty enough!" This is nothing other than an excuse. Get over it. You *are* pretty enough. You know you look good. It doesn't take much. You know you have good qualities, so play on them. If you can afford a day at the salon for new hair and make-up, go for it. A new hairstyle can do wonders. (Be sure to take notes on what the stylist is doing so you can do it later on.) And never underestimate yourself—never!

Each and every one of us has had our confidence tested at one time or another. *Get over it.* It's time. Find your confidence and nothing can stop you. If you think you're the best, you will portray that image and everyone else will think you're the best, too.

The question on your lips now is, "But how do I let him chase me without losing him?" You might be afraid that if you don't chase him a little you might not ever "get" him. Oh, boy. Listen to this: If you chase him and get him, you are setting yourself up for misery. The guy you get will never fully appreciate you because he didn't put any effort into it. There was no chase, no excitement for him. You just fell into his lap. That means he will never remember your birthday and he will do nothing but drive you crazy.

I have a friend who did this. She chased a guy down, got him and then got pregnant, trying to "trap" him. Guess what? He left her with the kid. He wants nothing to do with her now. And she can't seem to understand why. The main reason, obviously, is that he's an asshole. The second reason is she made it too easy on him and appeared desperate. It's the old "If they like me, there must be something wrong with them" situation that people sometimes find themselves in. No, it's not right and it's downright stupid, but some people do think like this. It's almost if you're too nice they think there's something wrong with you and they see it as desperation. No guy wants a desperate chick. Sorry, but it's true. Sure, he'll always use her and maybe even abuse her, but he will usually end up leaving her.

Obviously, that is an extreme example but I wanted to include it to get my point across. You have to realize that men do not like anything easy. Why do you think they don't stop and ask for directions? Because that would be *too* easy and they want to figure it out on their own. They want a chance to prove themselves. If you do their job for them, you've just put them in a very delicate position, one they will want to get out of almost immediately. Sure, he might stick around to get laid but as soon as he can find someone else to chase, he will.

Sorry, sorry. I know the truth hurts.

So how do you do this? How do you let him know you're interested so he can chase? All you need to know is that it's easy. Just show him enough interest to keep his hopes up and never be too bitchy. That means never cut to the bone with a comment about his mullet. (Let's hope he doesn't have one.) Just show him you have enough bitch in you so he won't walk all over you, but never too much that sends him running with his tail tucked between his legs.

It's that easy. When he approaches, all you have to do is engage in conversation but never to the point of taking it over. More on this later.

In a nutshell:

- Apply the supermodel principle with any man and see how well it works.

First impressions.

.

First impressions are important and this is how they work: Basically, when you first meet someone, if you start by putting yourself down, even by using self-deprecating humor, they will always view you as such. For example, if you say something like, "I have terrible hair. I can't do anything with it," that person will always look at you as the girl with bad hair. Even if you were just fishing for a compliment. That's why it's so important to always portray an image of self confidence. Self confident people never put themselves down in front of others. And other people rarely think badly of them. In fact, they're usually jealous of these people and that's because they know that person really and truly likes themselves.

Remember most people aren't looking for fault in others. Usually, it is us who projects our "bad" self images, including faults, on others. We give them what we want them to see and if we give them a bad impression, they will always view us as such. If you do this, stop. It's easy to stop. If you find yourself doing it, force yourself to stop. Maybe you use it as an icebreaker. No good. Don't use it at all and if you can't find anything to talk about besides how bad you are, then excuse yourself.

First impressions are important, just as everyone says. Use this time to your advantage. Giving an image of self confidence is like telling him that not only do you like yourself, but if he gets to know you, he'll like you too. A lot. That means he'll be glad he took the time to get to know you.

In a nutshell:

- First impressions are important. Use this time to project self confidence.

First Impression -
Go for :
confident
Friendly - smile
Listen
Laugh

A girl like you.

If you can just get over your hurdles, you will find a million reasons to get out there and find the man you want. As we've discussed, once you forget all that crap you've been told about dating and men and can wipe your slate clean, dating can be fun and exciting again. It was fun and exciting at one time, wasn't it?

Remember when you were younger and would go out? Remember how fun it was to flirt harmlessly with guys? Remember when you didn't know anything about "how" to do it? When you weren't looking for a steady date or a husband? Guys just fell all over you, didn't they? And they fell all over you because you were just being yourself.

That's right. That's the most important thing I, or anyone else for that matter, can tell you. Just being yourself attracts men like nobody's business. If they see you having fun and being free, they'll want to know what you're about. They will flock to you because you look carefree, which they will interpret as you won't expect much out of them. They want to join your party! But most importantly, they'll want to know what's up with a girl like you.

Learn to accept yourself and others will automatically accept you. Other people aren't trying to change you. You are. You are the one who wants to change yourself, not other people. Stop trying to change yourself because you were given a distinct personality. If you try to change it, it's only going to cause you trouble.

Never, ever give someone a false image of what you think they want. Always give them the real you, the true human being you are. So what if you get a little loud when you've had a few drinks? So what if you're shy and inhibited when you first meet a guy? So what if he doesn't like you? If he doesn't like you for who you are, he never will. And if he doesn't like you for you, he's not worth the trouble. If so, move on and you will find someone who does.

Once you can be yourself, then you can be a woman, like we discussed before. This is the most important thing in the book: *You have to allow him to look at you as a woman first and as a "person" second.* When he's looking at you, he's subconsciously sizing your genes up. Now don't get scared off because this is simple biology. He probably doesn't even know he's doing it. Whether you like it or not, you're doing the exact same thing to him, too.

So, just be yourself, the woman you are. If you've heard about how some men like overly aggressive women or really shy women or some other such nonsense, don't take it to heart. Never try to adjust yourself to meet his—or anyone else's—criteria. Always let things happen naturally. Don't try to be this or that because you think it'll work better. It never works better, believe me. So just be yourself.

In a nutshell:
- Be yourself. No need to be like anyone else or pretend.
- If he doesn't like you for who you are, he's not worth the trouble.

You're worth it.

What you're going to have to get in your mind is that you're worth it. And by this I mean, you're going to have to start thinking that these guys should be glad you're taking the time to get to know them. Never act desperate, i.e. "I've got him with me so I better do everything possible to keep him here."

Get it into your mind that you are one hot chick. Get into your mind that you deserve a good guy who will treat you right and do special things for you. Yes, you are worth having him make a fuss over you. Don't ever be afraid to ask for what you want. All anyone can do is say no and that's no big deal.

Still not convinced? Think of it this way: If you meet a guy and marry him, you are going to take on a more responsible role in the household. This may be a rude awakening for many of you, but it's very true. Things do change drastically once you tie the knot. And it's not all wine and roses.

So, therefore, you need to be as choosy as you can. You have a right to be picky. Not only will you be doing more housework than your husband, but you're the one that's going to give birth to the babies. That, in and of itself, should be reason enough to expect the best. This, however, does not mean waiting for a miracle guy. It means getting the best guy you can realistically attain.

This doesn't mean to be too picky. No, no, no! This means that you need to understand that you are a very valuable commodity. I hate to put it in those terms, but I don't know how to otherwise explain it. You've got what men want. All you have to do is tap into it and use it to your advantage. This starts by you believing that you are worth the effort. Guys should chase you. You are worth it.

After all, chasing is what he likes to do best. I know I keep saying this but I want you to get it into your head. Give him a run for his money. Let him be the man. Occasionally tell him how strong he is. Building his ego this way will make him look at you as "his" woman, the one he needs to protect, the one he wants to marry. A woman should play hard to get but never shut the guy down. Make it a challenge but not too difficult of one. Use discretion.

Men do want to get married. But they want to marry the "right" girl. After all, he has a lot to gain by getting married. He has way more to gain than you do. Maybe in the "old" days he didn't but today he certainly does. This means, once you get married, you're probably still going to keep your job. Not only that, but you're going to do most of the housework. If you have a baby, once your maternity leave is up, more than likely, you'll go back to work. And what does he do? He'll go to work, come home and plop on the couch. Think about this when you're out there.

Take all of this into consideration. If you think it's too difficult, then it may be for you. Sure getting married is fun. It's staying married that's hard. You want to get a man who you'll *want* to pick up after and remind to take out the garbage. You want a man who will treat you right. You don't want some guy you have to chase after. You don't want some guy you have to beg for a date. And you most certainly do not want a loser. What's the fun in that?

One more thing to consider—stop worrying that you might offend him. This means, don't guard yourself so much when you first meet a guy. Like I've said, don't ever be afraid to show him the "real" you. He should always be glad you're taking the time. Don't give a damn what they think about you. If they can't handle you, then they're not much of a man.

In a nutshell:
- Guys should chase after you. You're worth it.
- Make him work a little to get what he wants.
- It's going to be you who does most of the housework if you get married and give birth to the babies.
- He wants a chase. Let him have it.

Stop being desperate.

Before we go any further, let's get this out of the way. There's no easy way to say it, so I'll just put it out there: Stop being desperate.

This may or may not apply to you. Hopefully, it doesn't. But I have seen a lot of women who are willing to put up with a lot of crap from men when they don't have to. It's my opinion that they do so because they're simply insecure and don't think they "deserve" better. Therefore, they become desperate and let men walk all over them just because they have to have a date on Saturday night.

It's ironic, but once you stop acting desperate, you'll start getting the respect you deserve. You have to stop thinking you're not important. You are important. You've got what men want. So, there is no need for you to ever be desperate.

It's like this. If a woman chases a man and acts desperate, the man thinks there's something "wrong" with her. He also thinks the only reason she's chasing him is because no one else "wanted" her. Now, if she "catches" him and they end up married, they will both be miserable. He will always wonder why she chased him and she will always resent having to, mostly because he will treat her like crap. Desperation is very unnecessary. It leads to nothing but problems.

Yet, some women are desperate. Of course, we all have insecurity issues but when we let them stand in the way of our happiness and self worth, they begin to cheapen our very existence. When you're out there looking for the man of your dreams, you can't seem desperate. I've heard many women say, "But I don't want to end up alone!" Think about that. If you put some effort into getting a good, decent man, you won't end up alone. But if you reek of desperation, you'll end up with a jerk and then you'll wish you were alone. I've seen many women who end up with jerks and they are miserable. This, in and of itself, should tell you to never be desperate. As I've said, you're a hot commodity. Treat yourself as such and others will too.

Something to keep in mind is that when you do choose the man you want to be with, he will have a big influence on how the rest of your life turns out. First of all, if you meet and marry a bum, you will always have to support him. The man you marry can and will influence your life. Sometimes, it will be a good influence and others, not so good. I know a girl who married a guy and had a couple of kids with him. He was an okay guy, not really that ambitious or anything and he was very self-centered. She knew this going in and after they tied the knot, he wanted all the money to spend on his hobbies. He didn't care if the kids had new school clothes or not. It was all about him and his desires. Well, she decided enough was enough and got a divorce. However, he didn't want his gravy train drying up, so he contested the divorce and because it was so "stressful" to him, he got hooked on drugs. And then he got real mean. He started slashing her tires, calling her all kinds of names and abusing her in front of the kids and generally making her wish she'd never laid eyes on him.

I'm not trying to turn you off men or anything. I know not all men are low-life scum like this guy. But I do want you to realize that you have a right to be treated well by a man. So, it is very important to *not be desperate* and to be picky when it comes to choosing your guy. This isn't to say that you should pass on every guy or be afraid to be in a relationship. But do feel them out. And, whenever you find yourself feeling a little desperate to get some guy's attention, think of the above example.

It's your call. But know that you don't have to settle for the jerk and all you have to do is stop being desperate. Also, don't lie to yourself about a guy who doesn't want you. If he's playing games and leading you on, call him on it. Ask him this: "Is this relationship going anywhere?" And then let him answer honestly. If he doesn't want a relationship right now, then he doesn't. And that means it's time to move on. Never let him string you along. If he hems and haws, he's not serious and is probably just wasting your time.

If you find a guy and start playing that game of calling him all the time, you can expect one thing: He's going to get turned off. I don't believe there is anything wrong with a girl calling a guy every once in a while. But if you call him more than a few times a week after you first meet him, he's going to think you're desperate. Then he will either start treating you like crap—to get you out of his life—or simply stop returning your calls—ditto. Think of it this way: Do you like it when a guy bombards you with phone calls and never lets up? No, you don't and neither does he.

As I said in the previous chapter, you are worth it. You are worth a guy chasing you. So what if he doesn't call you back? Get out there and find someone who will and you *will* find someone else. There are a lot of men in the world and you don't have to settle for one that treats you like crap.

To be successful in dating, as with anything in real life, is pretty simple. But you must define what you want, what you're willing to put up with and the lengths you're willing to go. Or, better yet, what you're not willing to put up with and the lengths you won't go to.

Here's a guide:

- Have boundaries. Know what you will and will not "put" up with out of men. Is it okay if he's late? Is it okay if he doesn't call for days? Is it okay if he ignores you around his friends? Is it okay for you to be his booty call? If you're okay with putting up with this sort of behavior, then be prepared for this stuff to start happening.

- Never be afraid to tell men of your boundaries or if they've crossed them. This shows them that you're not willing to be a doormat. For example, if he starts talking sex right off and you don't like it, tell him to shut it or get lost.

- Know what you want out of a man, out of a relationship and out of life. Sit down one day and write it out, and be honest about it. If you want a white picket fence, then fine. If you want to play the field, then fine. But define it first. This way you won't waste your time with someone who doesn't want the same things as you.

- Confidence, confidence, confidence. When a girl is confident in herself and what she has to offer the world, nothing can stop her. A girl with confidence never reeks of desperation and that means men will like her all the more. A girl with confidence doesn't need a man, and when a man thinks you don't "need" him, he'll start "needing" you. Funny how that works.

- Know that every guy you meet isn't dying to settle down. Take these men with a grain of salt and have fun with them. But don't be brokenhearted if and when they break it off.

- Realize that any relationship you're involved in will be work. You have to be willing to work at it.

BE TRUE TO YOURSELF

It's important to have a guy who also understands this as well.

- Don't be afraid to pull the plug on a bad relationship—ever. Keep in mind if you end up married to someone who makes you miserable while you're dating, you will be even *more* miserable married. That's because once you're married, you get to start sharing stuff and spending all your "spare" time together. If you're not happy most of the time, then this might not be the one for you.

- And, lastly, don't be desperate. Don't be desperate to land a man and don't be desperate to keep one. We all know that great saying—and I'm paraphrasing—"If you love someone, set them free. If they come back to you, they're yours. If they don't, they never were."

That's a little cheesy, I know, but it's the truth.

The games people play.

Sometimes it just baffles me how stupid people have gotten over the years. It just baffles me how many people are willing to buy into the notion that there is a "better" way to date. The reason daters have gotten really stupid over the years, I believe, is because of the barrage of TV sitcoms about "singles", reality dating shows, romantic comedies, etc. Believe me, people in Hollywood have no idea how to date—they're all just trying to sleep their way to the top. Why would you want to take pointers from them anyway?

All this misinformation has lead to dating incompetence. No one knows what to do anymore. No one knows the "right" time to ask for a date or to kiss a person for the first time. It's not that hard to hook up or even to get married. People do it all the time. But, it seems, over the past few years, it's become an impossible task.

This whole dating game has been skewed. By doing this, we have thrown off the natural order of things, which makes everyone a bit crazy and agitated. Which makes it hard to meet and date and, possibly, mate. By people constantly changing the dating rules, it's made it hard for everyone else. That's what's wrong with dating these days. It's been messed with. It's been messed up! There are too many rules to learn and once you learn them, someone wants to change them again. There are too many parts to play—from being a wallflower to a raving bitch to a meek and mild Victorian. And, to top it off, we have to deal with everyone being a game-player these days.

You know what a game-player is, don't you? It's a person who has all sorts of stupid rules they've made up just to keep themselves distanced and unavailable. Presumably in case someone "better" comes along. Game-players are usually men. Sure, they are some women out there doing the exact same thing, but men outnumber them in vast quantities.

How to spot a game-player:
- He's fairly attractive.
- He will look around at all the other chicks while he's talking to you.
- He will most always try to get you into bed the first night he meets you.
- He will ask for your number and never call.
- If he does call, it's because you were second, third or fourth on the list. A girl he believes is "out of his league" is probably first and as soon as she returns his call, he's going to run to her. This means, you're on the "booty" call list. (Don't ever be on someone's booty call list. This is the most degrading thing to any woman. More on that later.)
- If you do date him for a while, he'll break it off as soon as you sleep together. Or he'll hang around for a steady lay and then break it off. But you'll still be on his "booty" call list. Lucky you.
- He's not looking for a relationship. He's just looking to get laid and have fun while he's "young".
- He'll probably invite you to a party of some sort, then ignore you once you're there. If you call him on it, he'll pretend he was "busy" or whatever and turn it around on you, making you feel like an insecure, petty individual.

- He will make your feel bad about yourself for a number of reasons. Mostly because it makes him feel good about himself. He'll also try to act hurt and wounded to make you feel guilty.
- He will never give you a gift of any kind—flower, birthday card, etc. and that's because you're unimportant to him.
- The only person he will ever love is himself.
- He's very immature.
- He thinks he's the hottest thing since sliced bread.

Game-players are usually attractive guys, many of which seem to have some sort of athletic background, i.e. he might have been a quarterback or whatever for his high school football team. Most of them are not movie-star hot, but they think they are and usually, because of this, everyone else thinks they are, too. They've got confidence because everyone has always told them how great they are. But they're not great guys. They're users who are always looking for someone better.

These guys will find any excuse to break it off with you once they get what they want. And, let's be crude, most of them just want some hot sex. They're not looking to get married and they are already in love with someone. That someone is themselves.

Dating a game-player will drive you crazy. You're never going to change this guy. Do you want a real man or a player? Do you want someone you can trust or someone who's going to emotionally bankrupt you? Remember, you're going to have to go by his rules.

If a guy, or a game-player, doesn't like you if you're a bit aggressive or a bit loud-mouthed, then to hell with him. That's right, say it with me: *To hell with him!* If you're too shy or too outgoing, then he can't handle you. This means, he's not right for you. Being a game-player is his excuse not to get to know you because you didn't fit inside some stupid mold he made up inside his head. For instance, he may think that a girl who kisses on the first date isn't "marriage material". Believe me, avoiding these guys will save you so much trouble it's unbelievable.

Besides, do you really want to be with a guy who will judge you so harshly if you give him a little tongue on a first date? I wouldn't.

But maybe it's not him; maybe it's you that's the game-player. How do you know? Well, no man has ever been good enough and there's always another one you want more. It's also called *not settling*.

If you are playing games, tricks or any of that other stuff in order to land the man of your dreams, what are you going to do if you get married to one of these guys you've played? He won't know who you are! You're going to have to keep it up for the rest of your life; otherwise, he's going to freak out when the "real" you shows up.

By playing mind games, you are only setting yourself up for failure. Don't be what you think he may want, be who you are. You were given a distinct personality for a reason, so use it to your advantage.

It's like this: If you see some guy and want to buy him a drink or whatever to open the conversation, then do it. Do whatever feels right *at that moment*. Don't fall for some stupid rule that might "set the precedent" for your future relationship. By talking with a guy, you're not asking him to marry you. You're just shooting the breeze. Talk to him and if nothing comes out of it, fine. Remember he can't play you if you don't play his game.

You want to be a man magnet, not a booty call. You want to attract good guys, not game-players. If you attract game-players, you need to get rid of them as soon as possible. These guys will do nothing but break your heart and cause you lots of misery. And isn't there enough misery in the world without them adding to it? If we all stop playing these games, these boys will have to end up playing it by themselves—or with each other.

So, do yourself a favor and stay away from game-players. These guys are trouble with a capital "T" and will use you until there's nothing left. And if you're the one playing games? Think of it this way: Playing games+get married=trouble. That should be enough to keep you off of it.

In a nutshell:

- Everyone's playing games. Stop playing games and maybe someone will want to play with you.

Bad boys and the misery they cause.

Along the same subject is the whole ideal of the "bad boy". He's a motorcycle riding, hard drinking, smoking guy. He's got tattoos and a bad attitude. And all women swoon whenever he's near.

I absolutely hate bad boys. Wanna know why? Because they're assholes. They think they are God's gift to women. They think just because they've got longish hair and a tattoo, they rule the roost. They are what's standing between a lot of good women and a lot of good men getting together. And they're standing there because women want them in the way.

Sure, on paper bad boys look good and they're always showing up on TV shows and in movies. In fact, they're quite desirable. They're a little moody and a little rough. Women think the bad boy will take her on a ride, preferably in the bedroom. And usually, they get what they want. But in the end, they get more than they bargained for when they see their bad boy chasing after another chick just like he chased them.

Because all women have bought into this notion of bad boys, these guys are getting worse and worse. Bad boys are trouble and not only do they cause a lot of trouble, but they sometimes stink. And they definitely stink up your life. Trust me on this, if you want a bad boy, you need to realize that you're not going to be the woman to "turn him around." The bad boy doesn't give a crap about your happiness and will get pissed off when you forget to bring beer on your way home from work.

In addition to that, bad boys are the worst game-players. They never want to settle down. They never want to fall in love or give anyone flowers. They want it all and, unfortunately, one day they'll wake up and realize they've pissed their lives away. Well, they won't wake up, but the woman who is with them will. Believe me, you don't want to be that woman. You deserve better.

Do yourself a huge favor and stay away from the bad boy. He's not worth the trouble.

In a nutshell:

- Forget bad boys. They're assholes who will emotionally bankrupt you.

The manchild.

In addition to being aware of game-players and staying away from bad boys, you might also want to take into consideration men who've never been married or in a serious relationship, i.e. the manchild.

If you're of a certain age—we won't get into numbers here—it might be impossible not to run across these men. But it's good to keep them in mind and to know what you're up against. Unmarried men over a certain age are to be handled with kid gloves. The age is irrelevant, but if he's over thirty-five and never been hitched or *close* to being hitched, use caution. If he ever says "I haven't had time to be in relationship" and he's not been on stranded on an iceberg for ten years, red flags should go up.

The manchild might be:
- A player.
- A loser.
- Damaged.
- A pest.
- Extremely insecure and overly sensitive.
- Crazy.
- A potential wife-beater.

A characteristic of the manchild is that they collect things, whether it be comic books, DVDs, old albums, sports memorabilia or what-have-you. They might still live in their parent's basement and dress the same way they did in high school—out of style. They keep themselves at about a twelve-year old mentality and always think women are bitches, though they frequent places like Hooters a lot. They are the kind of guys who are misogynistic and "rate" women on a scale of 1-10. They are all about hanging out with "the guys", normally in sports bars. In fact, they are totally obsessed with other men and with sports, almost to the point of being fanatical. Or closeted homosexual. They are guys who are "practicing" being men—they're not ready to be in a relationship just yet. They're still little boys inside and they like it that way just fine. In essence, they are Peter Pans who never, ever want to grow up.

Usually, you won't have to worry too much about these guys because they're not going to put out any effort to get a woman. However, they sure bitch and moan about how difficult women are and how "expensive" dating is. If you do happen to run across a guy with these traits, take heed. If he cancels a date in the first stage of the relationship to hang out with the guys, then he's a manchild. And that means he's not worth your trouble. Getting involved with one of these guys is a total waste of time from the get-go. Besides, who wants to get busy if mom and dad are at home?

In a nutshell:

- Be wary of the manchild. In fact, stay away until he decides to grow up.

Booty call?

This warrants mentioning. If you find that a guy has made you his booty call, you need to do one thing: Tell him to go to hell.

Being someone's booty call is probably the most degrading thing you can do. Sure, you might have fun, but it's not going to go anywhere. And he's just using you. When you are a booty call, all you are is a resource. It's like a guy is ordering a pizza when he calls you up for a booty call. He's looking at you in the same way he does when ordering a pizza. Why would any woman allow herself to be looked at in these terms? Why not just tell the world you have low self esteem?

If *you're* the one who's booty calling, the guy on your speed-dial probably thinks you like him and soon you two will have a relationship. Cut this out ASAP. Not only is bad Karma, but it invites diseases into your life—sexual diseases.

The booty call is dangerous territory. If you need release that bad, get a vibrator.

In a nutshell:
- Booty call? Just don't. Don't.

Pimps up, ho's down.

I have found a disturbing trend that I think deserves mentioning. In the past decade it seems as though women are relinquishing control to men more and more. I'm not sure where it comes from, but I have an idea that it's from the influx of rap videos and general "pimps" and "ho's" attitude that seems to be everywhere now. Men are pimps and women are ho's. This means, men can treat women like crap and get away with it because, as the pimp, they are in control.

Of course, this pimps and ho's attitude probably started as a joke. But it seems as though more and more women and men are taking it seriously and are going along with it. Men can put women on booty call. Men don't have to act like men; they can act like pimps and get away with it. In fact, men seem to be encouraged to act this way, whether it's from the media or their parents. Men don't have to stick around for a baby now. Men don't have to pay child support. Women are being left holding the bag—or the baby—more and more.

Pimps are up and ho's are down. Think about it.

Have you noticed that women are starting to get more and more plastic surgery not only to enhance their own looks but to look more like porn stars? It seems as though a lot of women are going very blonde and very chest-heavy. The clothing that they're wearing is so revealing it leaves nothing to the imagination. And if nothing is left to the imagination, then what's the point of titillation or even trying to find a good man? If you dress like this, he will always see you like this, as a potential ho. And men don't stick around to be with ho's.

It's harsh, I know. But the thing is, women are allowing this to happen. We're not teaching our young girls to respect themselves. We're allowing them to dress inappropriately and to behave inappropriately.

Women aren't demanding respect from men anymore. A lot of women are just glad some guy took the time to talk to them. That's pathetic! He should be glad you're taking the time to talk to *him*. But there's this sense of desperation now. I don't know why. Is there a man shortage or something? No, but there is a shortage of good men and that's because women are allowing men to treat them badly more and more.

Women need to take a stand and take back the power that they've willing relinquished to men. Men have no use for our power. When we give it away, they assume we're all "easy" and "unworthy" of treating well.

I have always said I would rather be alone than to be with a man who disrespected or abused me in any way. If you find yourself in a relationship where this happens more often than not, ask yourself if this is how you want to be treated for the rest of your life. Because life is short and it flies by.

If you demand respect, you will get it. If a man feels so threatened by you that he breaks up with you because you demanded to be treated well, he wasn't worth it. I know woman get desperate for a man after they reach a certain age, but no one should ever be *that* desperate. They created sperm banks for a reason, didn't they?

It's time for women to stop being doormats. Men have no right to treat women in the way I've seen. If it continues, men won't have to do anything for women in the coming years. And that's a shame because there is nothing like a good man.

If you find yourself in this sort of relationship with a man who treats you like a ho, do yourself a big favor and get out. Because, if you stay in a relationship like this, you will look back at it later and wonder why you allowed someone to treat you like this—for any length of time. What are you getting out of it? Nothing but being treated badly.

Start today by taking back your power. Don't ever hand it over to man. Keep it and demand respect. If you don't get it from someone, they are not worth your time. Once you believe this and apply it to your life, you will find that not only are you getting the respect you deserve, but you are a true man magnet. Remember, men don't want you to be easy, so don't be easy. And no one wants you to be a ho.

In a nutshell:
- Don't relinquish your control to a man.
- Demand respect.

Some universal truths to keep in mind.

Universal truths:

- Men are the aggressors. They like to chase. However if you're too hard to get, he's going to get frustrated and give up. So, let him know you're a little interested but not too interested. Then let the chips fall where they may.
- Give a signal. Once you spot a guy you'd like to know better, you will have to give him a signal to approach. This could be a smile or a simple "hello". More on this later.
- You can't make anyone fall in love with you. It doesn't matter how pretty you are or how many games you play, none of it matters. People fall in love because of mutual attraction and chemistry.
- You have to let nature take its course. After the introductions, don't tell him your whole history or push yourself on him or let him push himself on you. Sit back, relax and see where it goes. If it doesn't go anywhere, no harm done.
- Men love women who are themselves. They do not love bitches. They do not love women who are agitators and throw diva fits over too much ice in their drinks or something just as silly. Be cool, relaxed and just yourself and you won't have to worry.

- <u>Men back away from prissy women</u>. Being a goody-two-shoes ain't gonna cut it. If you snarl your nose at everything, he's going to back off, unless, of course, he's one himself. If so, you two should be very happy together.
- ~~Men don't like ice queens, either.~~ If you're cold and indifferent all the time, he's going to be cold, too.
- <u>Men don't understand women and probably never will</u>. It doesn't take a genius to figure this one out. This is the main factor that has kept us humans from dying out. There's a reason women drive men crazy. If we didn't, there might not be anyone around.
- <u>Men do not like overtly sexual women in the first stages of a relationship</u>. However, once you get together and establish trust, there is nothing better to do than let loose in the bedroom with your new guy. Blowing his mind at the right time is a one way ticket to getting him hooked on you.
- Sex on the first date equals bye-bye. Chances are, if he gets sex right away, he will have no incentive to get to know you. This sounds very old-fashioned, I know, but it's the truth.
- <u>Men want to get married as much</u> as women. As I've said, they want marriage because they have so much to gain from it. They just want to marry the "right" girl. Just like you want to marry the "right" guy. Good luck to both of you.

Let's take a look at you.

In order to be a man magnet, you have to look the best you can. Most women already have it together as far as hair, clothes and make-up goes. However, I want to go over a few things that can make you even more attractive to the opposite sex. As with anything, make your own rules to how you dress but use these simple guidelines. I know that this won't apply to everyone, and that's fine, so don't get your feathers up about it. Just take the suggestions that work best for you and tweak them to your own individual style.

While we are all naturally conformists to a certain extent, never be afraid to be a little sexy and stand out. (Keep in mind that sexy never means slutty, so don't overdo it.) Also, if your look is younger than your age, it's time to update. That means the Hello Kitty backpack has got to go.

Consider this:
- Are your clothes stylish?
- Could you lose a few pounds?
- Do you have big, scary nails?
- Are you dressing too young—or too old—for your age?
- Do you have big hair? (Be honest!)

Take all this into consideration. You want to look the best you can. The great thing about updating your look is that it doesn't take that much. I know women obsess over everything and I am certainly not going to add to anyone's anxiety, but the fact of the matter is, the better you look, the more likely you will attract lots of potential mates. The perk of being a woman is that it doesn't matter what kind of job you have. But, unfortunately, it does matter what you look like. Hey, I'm just trying to be honest here.

And no, I am not talking supermodel beautiful. Supermodels are as much a rarity as a super ugly person is. Everyone has a ton of good qualities. You can (on) build on the ones you have. You need to get yourself ready so that no man can resist your charms. It's easy. No plastic surgery needed. A little make-up, a nice hair style and a cute outfit usually does the trick. Remember, most guys are not that picky. (At least not as picky as most women.)

As I've said, it's not that hard to take what you've got and make it work for you. There are a few points to consider when you're doing a transformation, no matter how small, and it all starts by you looking in the mirror and in your closet to see what you can improve on. You want to be the best you that you can possibly be. Not only will this allow you to attract more men, but it will give you more confidence in everything you do. And by that I mean, the more confidence you have, the more chances you will be willing to take in life, whether it's applying for a new job, moving to a new place or approaching the guy you've had a crush on forever. Confidence is key and the way to gain confidence is to be the best you possibility can be.

Weight. I know this is a touchy subject, so please don't get pissed off. I also know society dictates that we're all too fat or too thin or whatever. I say, what each of us needs to do is stop listening to fashion magazines and get to the weight *that is best for our body type.* So, what you need to do is to go to a doctor, dietician or any other appropriate health professional and find out the best weight for your height and body type. Then try to get to it. Also, losing weight isn't that hard, so don't make it hard. It really is all about getting an appropriate amount of exercise. It's also about cutting calories and you do this by monitoring your portion sizes. However, *never* starve yourself to get into a size zero. (You'll only binge later on and that defeats the purpose. Besides, size zero is too damn skinny for any woman unless she is naturally a size zero and only a handful of women are.)

Keep in mind that, whether or not anyone wants to admit it, most men don't like super-skinny women. Not too long ago, I heard of someone who cheated on his wife. The reason he cheated? He said his wife had lost too much weight and he didn't find her sexually attractive anymore. He liked a woman "with a little meat on her bones" and she was just too skinny. Of course, this guy was a jerk, but I think what he said does have some credibility to it. Women put pressure on other women to be super-skinny, not men. Think about it. All you have to do is find the weight that is good for your height and body size and try to get there. I know this is hard but most times, being overweight is usually just masking some insecurity. Confront your insecurities head on and nothing can stop you.

Insecurity issues. Do you have insecurity issues? Find out by listening to what you say to yourself. If you find that you constantly put yourself down by saying you're not pretty enough or can never lose weight or can't do this or that, then you're insecure. No one but you can fix this. The best way to fix it is to stop looking for others to "complete" you. Stop fishing for compliments. Stop getting hurt if you feel slighted. Most times, other people aren't slighting you but you think they are because you're so insecure. Get over this and you can have any man of your choosing.

Hair. One of the first things a guy will look at is your hair. Men *love* long hair on a chick. Long hair on a woman spells youth, vitality and availability. Whether it's straight, wavy, curly or whatever, men love long hair. They don't love choppy, strange colored, punk rock hair. They may say they think it's neat or cool but given they choice, they'll go with the long hair any time. Sorry, punk rock girl, but it's true. Men love the natural look of long hair. When they see it, they imagine themselves running their fingers through it. So, if you have really short hair, consider growing it out but don't let it get stringy or too frizzy. Make it as luxurious as you can. Pay a little extra for a good color and cut but never, ever over-process it. And don't overdose on the styling products. If you can't run your fingers through it, neither can he.

Sometimes short hair does look good but not everyone can pull it off. You will need to go to a good stylist who is honest and will tell you what look best suits the shape of your head. This is very important. Some people just don't look good with short hair just as others look better with long. This is best left to a professional's opinion.

A note on going blonde: I don't do it myself, but if you do, be sure that you have the right skin tone for it otherwise, you can look sallow. And if you're not a natural blonde, you should realize that brunettes are just as sought after as blondes, as well as red heads. So, why not go natural? A woman I used to work with had bleached hair. I didn't see her for a while but the next time I did, she had gone back to her natural brunette. And she looked ten years younger! I was astounded at how good she looked. So, if you're bleaching your hair, why not give your natural color a try? It took years off her face so it might take years off yours. Besides, do you want to be with a guy who only likes blondes? If you marry him, you'll always have to bleach your hair.

Eyebrows. Now, let's get this over. Please don't get pissed off, but one thing all girls seem to be doing these days that makes no sense whatsoever is over-plucking their eyebrows. Sure, get your eyebrows waxed by a stylist or whatever, but never just have the one line over your eye. If you have this, stop it. A scary story—my mother over-plucked her eyebrows for years and now she can't grow them back. She has to use eyeliner pencil for the appearance of an eyebrow. Consider this next time you pick up the tweezers.

The over-plucked brows just makes women look older. Think about Lucille Ball. I read somewhere she shaved her eyebrows off and they never grew back. If you've plucked to the point of no return, go to a stylist and ask them to help you pencil in the best definition for your face. And if you can grow them back out, leave them alone and let them grow and then go to a stylist who can wax and shape them to make you look your best. Also, a natural looking eyebrow makes you look younger. So, maybe just tweeze a few stray hairs here or there and leave them to grow naturally.

Make-up. No war paint! You don't want to look like Bette Davis in *Whatever Happened to Baby Jane.* You want a natural look. Men do not like heavy make-up. I have never met one guy who told me he loved women with lots of make-up. So, go a bit natural, just some foundation and powder to even out your skin tone and just a little mascara to make your lashes stand out and a touch of red lipstick to make your lips succulent. (And, yes, red is the best color to use because it insinuates sexual desire.) I know some women wear too much make-up because of insecurity. If so, reread the paragraph on insecurity issues.

Nails. How about those nails? Well, just know that long nails look scary. You do not have to spend all kinds of money on tips and all that. Just let them grow a little, then buff them. Let your nails be natural. If you insist on polish, again, use a red or just a clear coat. Your toenails, however, can be painted a cherry red. This color goes with most skin types and *always* looks sexy.

Perfume. Never overdose on perfume. Just spray a little on your wrists and behind your ears. Overdosing on perfume is never a good idea because it doesn't allow your natural pheromones to shine through. Pheromones are one of the main things that attract men to women. This doesn't mean body odor, so don't freak out. You can use a little perfume, just don't go overboard. (And, of course, always use deodorant.)

Your clothes. We'll talk more about this in the next chapter, but right now all I want to say is that you should buy things that are classic and stylish. Never go too trendy. Always have a good pair of jeans, but just dressing in a pair of nice black slacks and a tank is good for running errands in. (You never want to leave the house in sweatpants or looking sloppy. You never know who you might run into.) You don't have to spend that much as long as your clothes fit well and accentuate your body nicely. Keep in mind that straight men don't care where you bought your clothes and they could care less what designer tag is on the inside.

It's funny but women spend all this time and money on make-up and clothes but men really don't care about this stuff. It's true. He doesn't care how much your purse cost or what designer shoes you're wearing and if he does, he might just be gay. In fact, most men would prefer you naked any day. I read somewhere that women don't dress to please men, but do it to compete with other women and to make other women jealous. This is definitely something to consider the next time you skip paying your electric bill to buy that pair of shoes. But when it comes to men, believe me, they don't care if you have a Gucci bag or not. Men don't care about that sort of stuff. Again, unless they're gay or bi-sexual. Or they're a cross-dresser.

In a nutshell:
- Take a look in the mirror and vow to improve in whatever area you can.
- If you have weight to lose and have had trouble, consider that it might be because of an insecurity issue. Confront the issue and the weight won't be that big of a deal to lose.
- Men love long hair, just don't over process it. Make it as natural and shiny as you can get it without chemicals.
- Over-plucked eyebrows make women look older. If you can grow them out, do so and then go to a stylist who can shape them.
- No long, scary nails. Leave natural and buffed.
- Stylish clothes that fit well and don't cost a fortune are the best.
- Never overdose on perfume.
- Never go out of the house looking sloppy. Never know who you might bump into.

Your man magnet outfit.

When you go out, you're dressing to attract a mate, right? And since this is the reason, you need to work it, girl. There is one type of outfit that all men love and is relatively easy to attain. It's an outfit that's sexy, yet refined, and can be pulled together in two shakes of a lamb's tail.

A man magnet outfit consists of:

- A nice button-down shirt or a form fitting sweater with a V-neck. You can wear this in white, blue or red. But not black or brown.
- A short black skirt. (Most important item you'll need.) Buy one that shows off your legs but if you want to keep it a little longer, buy one that hits right at the knees so he can still see your calves.
- A pair of stilettos—black pumps with a skinny heel. (These are the kind of heels models wear on the runway.)
- A pair of silver hoop earrings or a pair of diamond—or CZ—studs.
- Optional items: One nice bracelet and a nice watch.

This outfit is sexy but doesn't scream S-L-U-T! You never want your outfit to scream *slut* at a man because if you do, that's all he'll ever see you as. Men think in very black and white terms. A girl is either easy or she's not. She's either a slut or she's not. She's either girlfriend potential or she's not. Once you can understand that men don't really put that much into all this stuff, and see things in almost primitive terms, you can use this bit of information to the best of your advantage.

The reason you're wearing a shorter skirt is because it's *always* good to show a little leg. But don't wear the skirt so short it shows your ass cheeks. That's not what we're going for. He can see ass cheeks on the internet whenever he wants. Right now, you're covering the most delectable parts of your body so he'll wonder, "What does she look like naked?"

That's right. You want him to wonder but you're only giving him a little preview. Never the whole show! Never! (Well, at least not until you know he's worthy.)

Don't wear:
- Slutty clothes—too revealing outfits. Sure, the girl who wears this stuff might get hit on, but she's only going to get a one night stand for her trouble.
- Lots of jewelry. That means too many rings, earrings, bracelets, etc. It distracts from your natural attributes and is noisy.
- Never, ever wear pearls. Pearls give off the "grandma" vibe.
- Lots of make-up.
- Big hair.
- An anklet. Just don't.

Yeah, your man magnet outfit is that easy. Go get it and put it on and prepare to beat guys off you. Always remember, too, that clothing that is a little loose is always better than too tight. Buy clothes that are form fitting but don't show any fat rolls. (Yes, we all have a few.)

In a nutshell:

- Your man magnet outfit is stylish yet sexy. Keep it simple. Don't ever over-do your man magnet outfit.

Something to think about.

Hard truth: If he's going to fall in love with you, he's going to fall in love with you no matter what. This means, no matter what perfume or clothes you wear or how you style your hair. If he's going to fall in love, he's going to do it no matter what. Just give him a little time.

It's always been my opinion that guys pretty much know within the first few minutes of meeting a woman whether or not they're going to fall for her. Some of my male friends always argue with me about this, but I believe it's true. But I don't believe it's true because I'm a hopeless romantic. I believe it's true because I've heard so many men say, "I knew from the moment I laid eyes on her that I had to have her."

However, this doesn't mean he won't look at other women or even date a few here or there before he comes back to you. It means that if he's in love with you, he's in love with you and that means no one else can hold a candle to you.

So, in the end, it really doesn't matter what you do to "turn him off" or to "turn him on" for that matter. All that matters is that if he's worth the trouble, give him a fair chance. And always put your best foot forward.

In a nutshell:
- If he's going to fall in love with you, it won't make any difference how well you dress or how you act. But, of course, this is just my opinion.

God's gift to you.

God gave you something that makes every man on this planet go absolutely insane with lust and desire. Those two things make men's tongues wag and their loins ache. And what are they? Your boobs, of course.

Yeah, yeah, I know you're a feminist so don't get upset yet. Just sit back and listen.

The most important thing I can tell you is that if you want to be a man magnet you already have two of the most valuable assets at your disposal. Your breasts were given to you *in order* to attract mates. Knowing this can put you ahead of the pack. That's right. Your breasts or your tits or whatever you call them are your key to being able to attract just about any man, any time. Simply put, men love boobs. No, they worship boobs. Therefore, you should use any and every opportunity to show a little cleavage. Not too much, but just a peek. A good bra always takes care of this.

So, always wear a nice little outfit that shows off your breasts. Men love boobs and they will look at your chest before they look anywhere else. Don't ask me why, it's just a strange fact of life. (And don't get pissed off about it. You know it's true and there's nothing any of us can do about it.)

I know there are plenty of girls out there who will get upset when they read this. But to me, it's news worth knowing. And women would be well served to accept this fact of life. Men love boobs so much, they have all sorts of magazines dedicated to them. For some reason, many women see this as degrading. I don't and that's because if men didn't worship women to a certain extent, they wouldn't bother wanting to look at them in that manner. And that means they wouldn't bother with us at all. Men worship women's bodies. They are willing to do just about anything to see a glimpse of boob. This is good news, girls! This means we can have control simply by using what God gave us to the best of our ability.

Sure, it might not be "right". It might go against everything we've been taught, but the fact of the matter is that any man out there is going to be attracted to your body first and your brain second. Instinctively, we all already know this. We know this because it wouldn't make us so uncomfortable when we hear it if we didn't. I say don't be afraid to be your sexual self. If you allow your sexuality to shine through a little, men will flock to you. That's because men love women who love sex. I'm not saying to slut yourself out or anything like that, but don't be afraid to tap into your sexuality and use it to your advantage. That's what God gave it to you for.

Smart girls know this and smart girls use it. If you don't want to, then don't. A smart girl knows what she's got and will use it to her advantage. *Always.* And if that means using her sexuality to get what she wants, a smart woman will.

All of us are sexual creatures. However, it seems that women are supposed to discount their sexuality now. We're not supposed to use it to get a job or get ahead or anything. Well, all that depends on the individual girl. However when it comes to our personal lives, we *are* supposed to use it to attract a mate. The problem is, we've been told not to use it for everything else so that we've forgotten how to use it for what we're supposed to—to attract a mate.

Of course, I am not talking about sleeping your way to the top or wearing clothing that is too revealing and makes you look like a ho. I'm talking about using it just a little to get what you want. Tap into it. Right now. Tap into your sexuality. Men's minds are always on sex. If you can get his mind on you—in that manner—he'll do anything because he can't wait to get his paws on you. Keep in mind that you've got something he wants, so make him work for it. And let's face it. His main goal from the moment he meets you is to get you into the sack.

And once they see your cleavage, they'll want you. It's like boobs trigger something deep in their brains and makes them wake-up. Always remember you have what you need to attract a man. And it's sitting on your chest.

Even if you don't have much on top, you still have something that drives men crazy. And, no, you do not have to get a boob job in order to use this to your advantage. If you have small breasts, you can be a bit more daring and go without a bra. Once a guy gets a peek at a nipple, he's done for and he won't care how small they are. Of course, you're only going to do this while you're out hunting a man. You're not going to go without a bra to the office. (It's always important to use your brain when it comes to things like this. Never put yourself in a position of getting fired.)

In a nutshell:

- God gave you two great gifts. It would be a shame not to use 'em. So, don't be afraid to use them to your advantage.

Titillation.

Titillation is the key to getting a man interested in you. It's what you do to inspire him to chase. It's something that you are quite capable of. And all you do is tap into your sexuality. It's not about slutting yourself out. However, in order to attract men, you are going to have to let them know—in a very titillating way—that you are available. You are going to have to let them know that you're ready for a guy like them. Titillation means always keeping their minds on sex. Well, it's already there most of the time, but you can help a little. And once you can get their attention in this way, you can keep it for some time afterwards.

How to titillate:
- Tiptoe to get a kiss, then pull back and smile.
- Unbutton your shirt to *there*. Yes, to *there*, which is where their eyes will be all night.
- If you're eating Chinese or Italian, slip a noodle into your mouth provocatively.
- Let him feed you off of his fork, then chew as you look into his eyes. End with a, "Mmm…that's good! Can I have another bite?"
- When you go out to dinner, eat. Men love to see women eat. They think that a woman who likes to eat also likes to…well, she probably likes sex. Don't order a watercress sandwich or pick at a salad. Order a steak and eat it like you enjoy it, but do it like a lady and never like a truck driver.

- Always lean in towards them when you're talking, as if you want to get your point across. This will make him take notice of you even if there's a supermodel across the room. And why does it make him take notice? Because you're right there in front of him and a bird in hand is always better than two in the bush.

But do all of this like its second nature. Practice at home if you have to. You don't want to come off as being a fake and if you're not comfortable doing it, you will. Practice your craft and hone it until you can do all this stuff like it's second nature.

One more thing. Take your time. Ease into all this. God gave you everything you need to get a man—or a lot of men. And—this is very important—don't act nervous even if you are. Always play off confidence, even if you don't have it yet. Act the part and soon you will *become* the part. It's the whole idea of "fake it until you make it", so fake not being nervous and soon you won't be. Keep in mind that it just takes a little time to get you at that level. Soon, it will become easy. And you'll be unstoppable.

In a nutshell:
- Titillation is a great way to make a guy go crazy. So, drive him crazy. He'd do the same to you if he had a set of tits.
- Fake it until you make it.

Equals?

Let's go ahead and get this over with. You might be thinking, *Acting like a sexy woman is all well and good, but shouldn't men and women be equals?*

Sure, in everyday life you can be. But in a relationship, it's give and take. If he can't do anything for you—like giving you a mind blowing orgasm or fixing your computer—then why would he want to pursue a relationship? If you already have everything figured out, why would he bother?

I don't believe a relationship is ever truly equal but I do believe that each person can give one-hundred percent of themselves *to* the relationship. So what if he always takes the initiative to have sex? So what if you spend all the money on new shoes? See what I'm getting at? Equality is a great word, but it does confuse us. Don't get hung up on issues that really aren't relevant to relationships. And equality doesn't belong there. You will always end up doing more housework and he will always have to mow the yard. It's give and take in a relationship but never really equal in a "tit for tat" sort of way. The key is to let go of this and find out what works best for you.

If you get hung up on always wanting to be equals, then life becomes less fun. I say let it go. What you're after in any relationship is mutual respect. As long as you respect each other, you will have a good relationship.

I once read an article on one of the pioneers of women's publishing. This woman was married to the same guy forever and every morning she got up and fixed him breakfast. He said he didn't really want her to, but she wanted to, it made her feel like a woman who was taking care of her man. She was a woman at home and a tiger in the business world. That was her balance.

My advice? Have him fix you breakfast. You're worth it, aren't you? And on other days, you can fix him breakfast. It's all about achieving a balance.

In a nutshell:
- Forget about being equals. It's too much trouble to keep score. As long as he respects you and you respect him, you'll be fine.
- It's all about mutual respect.

Sexy yet approachable. In other words, act like you just don't care.

It's all in your attitude. I know everyone says this but it's true. If you want to be a man magnet, you will be. If you waffle, you won't.

Men approach women who they feel are approachable. If you put yourself out there as unapproachable, they'll usually stay away. Unless they're pests, of course.

The key to becoming a man magnet is confidence. Sounds too simple, but it's true. Men love women who are self confident, just like women love men who are self confident. And, just like women loathe men who lack confidence, men loathe women with issues. So, never bring your "issues" on a date. You can save all that for later when you're seriously dating.

So how can you be confident? While we've discussed this in the "A girl like you" chapter, it's important to keep in mind that you must think of yourself as someone who is worth a guy making a fuss over. Like he should be glad you're taking the time. This doesn't mean that you should act like a bitch, but it means to be a little flirty and nice and only *slightly* interested.

If you're afraid of coming off as a bitch because you're a little aggressive, then try to just sit back and listen at first. Just relax. Some women are just naturally aggressive and that's fine. However, you need to find a way to tone it down. Never be too aggressive—it scares men away. They have to "think" they're in charge. It's not true, of course, but you can let him "think" that it is. Just tone it down a bit at first and listen to what he's saying. (Or, at the very least, pretend to listen.)

Another man magnet secret? You act like you don't care about men. If they come over, fine. If they buy you a drink, fine. If they don't? Fine. This means you're a free spirit. You're not waiting on someone to ask you to dance. You're just there because you like to go out. If you can develop the attitude of "I just don't care", men will want to know what's up with you. It always works.

That's a hard fact of life, but it's true. The less you seem to care, the more they want you. All this can make a person go utterly insane but if you can learn to work this to your advantage, you can pretty much have any guy you want. Think of it as reverse psychology and if you use that, you will be unstoppable.

Men, to a certain extent, don't want to figure women out. They want us to keep them guessing. If we keep them guessing, then we become what is commonly known as a "mystery". If we lay everything out on the table with a guy right off the bat, then we've become a pain in the ass. You don't want to become a pain in the ass. This means, don't tell him that much about yourself at first. It's always good to retain an air of mystery.

Most importantly, remember to act like you just don't care. Throw him a smile to approach, but then go right back to whatever you were doing. When he comes over, say "hello" and then wait for him to respond. Take your time. Ease into it. Don't think just because he's there that you have to talk his ear off. Let him open the conversation and let him ask you questions about yourself. If he's shy and fumbling over his words, go easy on him and ask him questions. More than likely, he will want to know every single thing about you and all at once. Don't give in to ego and tell him everything. Just smile, answer his questions and then ask him something

If, for some reason, his attention starts to wane during your initial conversation, do yourself a favor and walk away. Don't ever get hung up on one guy. Be confident enough to say "see ya later" without it ruining your life. No one likes rejection of any kind, so if you cut him off first, you don't have to suffer from it. More than likely, this will leave him wondering about you. He'll wonder what he did and he'll wonder what kind of girl you are. You're the kind of girl who doesn't take crap, that's the kind of girl you are. Never forget that you are in control, even if he's the aggressor. Never forget you can get what you want. Yes, it's that easy. Just don't be shy about asking for it. By walking away from a knucklehead, you're showing the world you're not going to put it with any crap. If you do these things, you can have your pick. Men love a challenge. If you challenge them, they will do anything to get what they want and what they want will be you.

Another thing. Don't make marriage your goal, or at least don't make it known to him when you're first getting to know each other. In fact, I wouldn't mention it until they do. Not only can guys smell desperation but they will run like the wind if they do. Instead, just get to know this new guy. For all you know, you won't want to marry him. Just relax and have a good time. Not every guy you meet you'll want to marry, believe me. So get the marriage goal out of your head for now and just be who you are. And who you are is a girl just out and about looking for a good time.

Of course, marriage is a very legitimate goal, but don't show any sort of interest in at first. You might find you can't stand this new guy and if you talk marriage and he wants it, then where will you be? Besides that, take this time to not only get to know a few new fellas, but get to know yourself as well. Find out what kind of guy you really like to spend time by spending time with a few. Remember, you never have to settle on the first guy you meet.

On the other hand, don't let *him* be too aggressive. If he comes on too strong and is making you uncomfortable, tell him to back up. And you don't have to be a bitch to do this. Just tell him, "Would you mind not doing that?" He'll get the point. If he's being really aggressive this means he's into you and he doesn't want to let you get away. But he can sometimes come across as being overbearing. Like I said, all you have to do is tell him to back off. This doesn't mean being a bitch, though.

That's pretty much it. If you can act like you just don't care, you will become unstoppable. And being unstoppable is pretty darn fun.

In a nutshell:
- Act like you just don't care.
- Practice flirting.
- Don't make marriage your goal. (If it is, keep it under your hat at first.)

The bitch is back.

I believe the subject of being a bitch warrants mentioning. Some women think the worse you treat a guy, the better he will be to you. Not so. Men do not like bitches. They don't like someone who is constantly putting them or their friends down. They don't like someone who is constantly picking at them or making them feel uncomfortable. They also don't like to be yelled at or made to feel inferior.

Being a bitch and being a woman who doesn't take crap from men are two very different things. You have to achieve a balance but you might have to adjust for each guy you go out with.

Women who are bitches find ways to put their men, and everyone else, down. They do it to feel good about themselves, not because they want respect. By belittling others, they can think more highly of themselves.

Women who stand up for themselves respect themselves and others. They know that by doing this, they are telling the world they're not going to take anyone's crap. They know when to do it and they do it without sounding harsh. However, they're not afraid of sounding harsh. But they won't be bullied and they won't be doormats.

It's good to keep in mind that while men don't love bitches, they do love a woman who's not afraid to put them in their places. They like to know that you won't take their crap. They want to know they can't "run all over you". Why is this such a big deal to men? To have someone put them in their places? Because most men have one woman in their life that was never afraid to put them in their place and they love her for it. And that woman is their mother.

Don't freak out. Just listen.

Men like women who put them in their places. Sure he might look at it like this, "Oh, she's so little and cute and here she is telling me what to do," but he's always going to be comparing you to the most important person in his life and that's his mom.

Sounds weird, but it's true. Treat him like a child from time to time and he'll be in heaven. He'll know when to tow the line and if you let him know that you are a woman who sometimes needs help, he'll know he's still in charge of some things. Besides this, he knows if a woman isn't afraid to speak her mind, she won't be afraid to get busy in bed. That's it. That's why. They want to know that you won't kowtow to them.

I'm not saying you have to be his mother. That's not what this is about. I'm saying don't be afraid to put him in his place, just like his mom always does. Don't be afraid to tell him if he's stepped out of line. And more than likely, he will from time to time. Get prepared for it.

In a nutshell:
- Men don't like bitches.
- Men do like women who aren't afraid to put them in their places.

Mama's boy?

One of the best ways to see how a man will treat you is to watch how he treats his mother. So, if at all possible, check out how he treats his mother. This is the biggest indicator of how he's going to treat you.

If a man treats his mother with dignity and respect, he will treat you that way as well. If he treats his mother like crap, he will treat you like crap, too. So, my suggestion to you is if you find a guy you really like, observe they way he treats his mom. You can do this by saying, "I'd love to meet your parents soon." (You should be "seriously" dating for at least a month or two before you do this.) If he agrees, offer to cook dinner for them and watch how they interact with one another. If they have a caring relationship, this woman has done a good job with her boy. If there is tension or he whines around her, she's probably not done such a good job. This means, he will soon start whining around you. This also means he probably blames her for all the wrong in his life and will eventually seek therapy.

However, if he's a little *too* close to mom, he might just be a mama's boy. Mama's boys are tough ones. Sure, many men are mama's boys to a certain extent and they allow mama to give advice and cook them the occasional dinner. She's also allowed to pinch his cheek at any time. This isn't that bad. It's just when they allow mama to control their lives that things get a little hairy. I mean, scary.

How to tell if he's a mama's boy:

- He lives at home with mama.
- He can't go anywhere without first letting mama know.
- When he goes on vacation, he has to call mama first thing to let her know he's arrived and how long he plans on staying.
- He calls her at least once a day.
- He asks for her advice on dating.
- He calls her his best friend.
- She still buys his clothes.
- She still cleans his room.
- Mama has never approved of any of his previous girlfriends.

This sort of mama's boy is bad news. Avoid.

In a nutshell:

- Check out how he treats his mom. It's a good indicator of how he will treat you.
- If he's a mama's boy, ask him when they plan on cutting the umbilical cord.

Sending signals.

Once you've spotted a guy you'd like to get to know better, it is imperative that you send a signal that you're interested. By this I mean, throw him a little smile or, if he's close enough, say "hello" first.

I know there are many dating books out there that tell us to never approach a guy. Well, you're not approaching him by smiling or saying hello, you're sending him a signal that you'd like him to come over and approach *you.*

You have to keep in mind that every single man out there isn't a cardboard cutout of what dating books and TV present. There are tons of guys who are shy or inhibited and shake in their boots when approaching women. As I've said, men are the natural aggressors when it comes to courtship but for some of them, they can't get over the idea that you're going to turn them down. Some men break into hives when they spot a girl they'd like to talk to. If they do this, they're not going to approach you. And that's because it's just too painful for them to do this even if that means they have to let the opportunity pass them by. This is why I'm saying, why not make it a little easier on him and approach him with a friendly smile? I don't think there's any harm in that.

If you want to let him know you're interested, just send him a signal. That's all you have to do. A casual, "Hello" could do the trick or a friendly smile. When you get ready, know that you don't have to be blatant and put out a banner. A small smile, a flip of the hair, all those things that are ingrained in us to attract the opposite sex are exactly the kind of things that work. Steal a few glances his way.

Believe it or not, this works. Unless he's a complete jackass, he will know you're interested. And if he doesn't approach you out after you've sent the signal? Don't worry about it. You haven't been rejected. You've just saved yourself a lot of trouble.

Take this case-by-case. Just like women, all men are different. Some are very aggressive and some are very inhibited. The more you are aware of this, the better you will be at reading people and this is a skill everyone should have. I've known men who really wanted to get to know me but were so shy their faces would go red anytime they were around me. That meant, I had to approach, otherwise it just wasn't going to happen. Even if they are dying to, they won't. You have to get that into your mind and get out all that other stuff about being too "aggressive". You're not being aggressive in a case like this, you're being open to possibilities.

So, be aware that you will more than likely run across some of these guys. That's okay. If you have to open the conversation, then that's what you have to do. And don't be afraid that by doing this that you're setting the precedent for the entire relationship. Some guys just need a little nudge, that's all. Give it to them and be willing to let them take over when they get more comfortable around you.

And besides that, you know instinctively when a guy likes you, all women do. How do you know? He will give you "the look" and then he'll look away. And when you catch him looking at you again, you get that funny little feeling in your stomach, right? Right. That's how you know he likes you.

So what if you throw him a signal and he ignores you? Well, truthfully, he wasn't that interested. The worst that can happen if you throw him a signal and he doesn't respond is that he just doesn't respond. No biggie. Move on and don't take rejection personally. Once you can learn to do that, you are going to be free to do whatever you want to do. You have to know that most times, rejection in this form has little to do with you and more to do with the person doing the rejecting.

Remember, if he rejects you, he could be:
- Gay.
- In a heavy-duty relationship.
- Heartbroken over some other chick.
- A misogynous bastard.

If he's any of the aforementioned, why would you want to deal with him anyway? You wouldn't and by him "rejecting" you, you've saved yourself a bundle of trouble.

In a nutshell:
- Send the guy of your liking a signal.
- A signal doesn't take that much. Just a nice smile thrown into his direction or a "hello".

Availability.

This leads us to the subject of availability. When you're out, you need to make sure the guy you like isn't already taken. There is a good chance that some of the men you meet won't be available. There are also a few other factors to keep in mind, too.

These kinds of guys are off limits:
- Married. (Obviously, look out for a wedding ring. Or a tan line where a wedding ring should be.)
- Just divorced. (One to six months after a divorce chances are he's still smarting and if he's not smarting, he's playing the field or on the rebound—avoid.)
- In a heavy relationship.

These guys can't and won't commit to you. Forget about 'em. You will need to learn how to weed them out. And how do you weed 'em out? After you've talked with him for a few minutes and you're still not sure if he's available, come right out and ask him, "Are you seeing anyone right now?"

And be warned, this guy could be married and out to cheat on his wife. He could lie and tell you he's available. How to tell? He might act slightly nervous and avoid your question about his availability. If you're suspicious, you should just flat-out ask him if he's married and don't beat around the bush. This way, he won't be prepared for your question. It's a lot harder to lie this way. If, for any reason, he says he's not and you're still suspicious, avoid him. This is your gut instinct telling your something is up with this guy. Listen to it.

Sure, sometimes women do date married men. Who knows why? All I can tell you about this is that if you do it, you will bar yourself from getting an available man. That's because all of your time and emotion is going to be zapped with Mr. Married Guy. Do yourself a big favor and avoid this situation. Even if he is movie star handsome and promises to leave his wife. You need to know that he's just lying to get in your pants and once he does that, he won't need you any more. Besides that, if you get married on down the road, your husband might do the same thing to you. It's called Karma. Do yourself a favor and don't have anything to do with a married man.

Oh, yeah, be sure to avoid the other two types of guys as well. They're just out to get into your pants.

In a nutshell:

- It might be a good idea to ask if the guy you like is seeing someone else. Sometimes he might be.
- Never date a married man. Remember, he's cheating on his wife and if you ever get married, Karma could come right back and bite you.

The quandary: Can a chick ever ask a guy out?

I am so sick of this question. Why don't we just all come out and say what this question really means? It means: "If a chick asks a guy out, doesn't that mean she's desperate and *has* to ask him out?"

Hmm… Let's take a closer look at this. Desperate? No. Putting herself at the risk of seeming desperate? Yes. Some books will tell you that if you ask a man out, then you're asking for trouble. I agree, somewhat. But the only problem with that is that some men are so shy that they just can't bring themselves to ask women out, like I discussed before.

I think you should take this on a case by case basis. If you find a guy who's shy, why not make the first move? The only thing he can do is say no. However, if you have a guy who's not shy and is not asking you out, it might be because it never occurred to him to ask you out. That could be a good thing or a bad thing. It might not be because he doesn't desire you but maybe he thought you were out of his league or perhaps already involved with someone. Always remember that men have issues with insecurity just like women.

I say, what could it hurt? One of the major problems with the relationships between women and men is that neither of us want to make the first move. *If he liked me, he should ask.* And, on the other side, *If she was interested, she would let me know.*

Again, neither one of you is getting any younger. You could play this little game for eons and still not get any closer to getting what you want. The fact of the matter is, and feminists can burn me at the stake for saying this, women are in control for most of the relationship, so wouldn't it stand to reason that they are in control of it getting off the ground in the first place? Yeah it makes a helluva lot of sense to me.

In a nutshell:
- There are plenty of guys out there who are shy and need that little push to get them going.

Where to meet him and get his attention.

Are you ready to meet someone that you're going to make very happy? Let's get to it, girl. You can meet a guy in a number of places. Once you're dressed in your man magnet outfit and ready to go out, you're not going to have to worry about attracting guys. That's because they will be drawn to you. Remember, you're now comfortable in your own skin. You're a hot chick and you can have your pick of the guys. You're sexy yet approachable. You have a great smile and know how to converse.

The thing to understand is that it doesn't take that much for any woman to get a guy to talk to her. Want to know what works best? Saying "Hi" to the guy you'd like to get to know better. And if you say it with a smile, you're home-free.

You don't think it's that easy? Why not give it a try? You are going to have to get used to the idea that as women, we have *the power* in our hands. The problem is we've dampened it for so long we've forgotten how to use it. Learn to use your womanly wiles and you can have any man you want. Learn to use everything you have: Your smile, your body, your brain, everything and no man will be able to resist you.

Places to meet men:
- Parties.
- Bars.
- Clubs.
- Restaurants.
- Museums.
- Grocery stores.
- Video stores.
- Bookstores.
- The post office.
- The train station.
- Just about anywhere in public.

Let's say you're going out for a drink with the girls, shall we? (It's a good idea to always have a few lady friends go with you when you go out. If you don't have a lot of female friends, see my suggestions below.)

Say you see a guy you want to get to know better in a bar but he's oblivious to you. Not to worry. Try to catch his eye and then throw him a smile and see what happens. But what if you can't catch his eye? Do something stupid like bumping into him. This is the oldest trick in the book but it works.

Another great trick is "Do you have the time?" That's all you have to do—ask him what time it is. (Make sure that you are either setting your watch or that you're not wearing one.) This is sometimes better than the bump.

He should be pleasantly surprised that a hot chick like you could be so clumsy or doesn't know the time. Now, force yourself to smile. The smile is the biggest conversation opener in the whole wide world. It works like nobody's business. It shows that you are interested in him without you having to come right out and say it. Now the next move is up to him. He should ask if you'd like a drink or what you're doing in a place like this or whatever. (His reaction will be different for each place you encounter him in. Obviously, if you're in a grocery store, he's not going to ask you if you'd like a drink.)

Now, if he doesn't ask you if you'd like a drink or show any interest, smile at him and then excuse yourself and go to the ladies room or wherever. And forget about him. But what if you still want to talk to him? Listen to me. If you sent him a signal and he didn't respond, he's not responding because he's not interested. Forget about him and concentrate on someone else. Also, keep in mind that he might not be available and that's why he's not responding.

And it shouldn't matter if he doesn't respond. As I've said, once you've got confidence and have on your man magnet outfit, guys will be clamoring to talk to you. So what if you run across a few who don't want to chat? Big deal. If, however, you want to "make the first move" for whatever reason, then do it. I mean, do whatever you feel is right at that moment. If you'd like to talk to him but can't seem to get his attention, then go up to him and talk to him. You'll need an opener, though.

A few icebreakers:
- "Do you have the time?"
- Compliment him on something, like his watch or shirt.
- "Hi, how are you?" (Always, works the best.)
- All icebreakers should be said with a disarming smile.

A note on a shy guy who doesn't talk much: When you come across these guys—and you will occasionally—be nice and try to draw him into conversation. Maybe compliment him on his watch or shirt. Smile and let him know you'll stay and chat for a few minutes. Once he knows this, he should relax and start talking. Always keep in mind that some men are painfully shy. They want to talk, it's just hard for them. So, be gentle with these guys and be aware that he might stammer and act foolish. This is not a bad sign! It just means he's nervous. You're probably nervous too. Take a breath and force yourself to have a little conversation. If he's a good guy, he's going to want to talk. He might stammer, as I've said, but he's not going to flee. If he flees, then he's not worth it.

As you're talking, try to find a few things in common. Ask him when his birthday is and see if you have the same sign. Or comment on the fact that you're both wearing the same color shirt. Anything, just find a commonality.

And let nature take its course. If he's interested in you, he should eventually ask for your number. If he's not, he's not going to. Sorry. I know that's hard to hear, but it's true. Believe me, if he likes you, he's not going to let you get away without getting your number unless he's totally clueless. If you believe he is totally clueless, why not offer your number?

One last thing. If you have trouble meeting men, why not try to make some new *girl*friends? Girlfriends can bring in those dates like nobody's business. Everyone has a spare brother or cousin around to set you up with. And if they don't, you can always talk them into going out with you to someplace new where you could meet someone new.

How do you make new friends? I know it can be a hassle once you're all grown up. But if you want to make new friends, you can approach women at work, join a gym, or take a cooking class. Just engage people who you have something in common with in conversation. This is a good way to make new friends. You can also do some community service such as volunteering in a soup kitchen or for Habitat for Humanity or something like that. This will open you up to meeting all kinds of new people. Not only that, you're helping someone else as you help yourself which is a great way to put Karma in the bank.

There are lots of ways to meet people, so don't be intimidated. I know it's sometimes harder to make girlfriends than man friends, but it's definitely worth a shot.

In a nutshell:
- Get his attention by throwing him a smile.
- You can also do the "bump" thing.
- Or you can ask him what time it is.
- Always use an icebreaker to start a conversation.
- Why not meet some new girlfriends who might be able to set you up?

When he calls and how to give him a chance.

When he calls to ask for a date—and why else would he be calling?—tell him sure you'd like to go with him. Now you can play that game of having a "scheduling conflict" if you want to. This game is also called "playing hard to get". But if you really like the guy, don't do it. Sure, make him sweat it for a couple of minutes but eventually tell him you'd like to go on a date. Of course, never be too eager at first and squeal like a little girl. Just stay calm and collected even if you're feeling butterflies.

Sure, you can make him wait a little while to see you and it will put you in his mind more, but the thing is, if he's not that interested or thinks you're being too aloof, he's not going to call back and ask for another date. It's your call but remember you are a man magnet. You don't play games. You grab life with gusto. If he wants to play games with you and thinks you're too "easy" by accepting a date so soon, then he's weird. He should be glad you're taking the time to even talk to him. If you don't want to play games, accept his date.

When you go on your date, keep in mind that he's going to be nervous and you will need to give him a chance. So, don't keep score and don't judge him. Be nice! Allow him to make a few mistakes. Don't totally write him off if he forgets to unlock your door or hold the door open. Then again, he may be too eager to please and do so much at first that it annoys you. (Remember, he is a man and this won't last. Enjoy it while it does.)

You will have to keep in mind that guys get really nervous when going on dates and/or trying to meet women. If he's acting weird—but not creepy—it might just be because he's nervous. I've witnessed this many times. So, give him a disarming smile and ask him to tell you a little about himself.

Not every guy you meet is going to dig you and vice versa. Take time to get to know this guy, this person, this human, just for that space of time. Don't expect anything to come out of it. If you get to know him and he tells you—or you find out—that he has done dorky stuff or gone to dorky events like *Star Trek* conventions, don't pass judgment and say to yourself, *Loser!* This might be something he did in college for fun. Big deal. Don't freak out if you find he has a stamp collection or any other geeky thing. Who cares? Most guys have done something geeky at least once in their lives. Besides, everyone knows about *your* Barbie doll collection.

So, be kind to him. Go easy on him. *Allow him to be human.* This, in turn, will allow him to allow you *your* mistakes. You're not perfect, are you? No and none of the rest of us are either.

In a nutshell:

- Accept his date if you don't want to play games and get the show on the road.
- Give him a chance and overlook anything in his past that might make you think, "Loser!"

Dealing with a cheap bastard.

Some men, unfortunately, are cheap. They don't "think" they have to pay for dinner or bring a girl a flower every once in a while or do anything at all to make her feel special. These men are not worth your time or effort.

Don't ever offer to pay for dinner or go "Dutch". If he can't afford to take you out, then you don't want to be with him anyway. He has to at least be able to afford dinner and a movie. Believe me, if you get any guy who can't afford that, then you are better off alone. The guys who want women to pay are usually going to start asking for money and if they can crash in your spare room. Stay away from these guys!

Feel him out. If he doesn't pick up the check and you like him, give him a hard look as you're putting down your part of the check. Then say, "I don't think this is going to work." When he asks why not, say, "I don't like cheap men." If he whines about this being a double standard, give him a piece of your mind. Who does he think he is?

Think of it this way: If you married this guy, he would continue to be cheap. In addition to that, do you really want to spend your life with a man who will ask why you need so many shoes? I'm not saying to not give a cheap bastard a chance, but if he doesn't have any other endearing qualities—handsome with a great sense of humor—getting over the cheap factor will take some getting used to. There has to be something that makes up for his cheapness.

Maybe he doesn't have any money. Does he look poor? If you're dating a poor guy… Well, do you want to marry someone you will always have to "keep up"? Think about it before you invest any time. Being poor and being a bum are two entirely different things. If he's poor and has potential—maybe he's waiting for his "big break"—make it up as you go. Don't cut out the poor guys, just the cheap ones. But keep in mind even poor guys will insist on paying for your dinner if they're worth having. Even if that dinner just consists of a Big Mac and fries.

Of course, if your relationship progresses, you will probably want to treat him sometime. But during the beginning stages, let him do the treating. You're worth it, girl.

In a nutshell:
- My advice in dealing with a cheap bastard is always the same: They're not worth it.
- Make it up as you go if you get involved with a poor guy with potential. (Never know, this guy could turn out to be president of his own company or a movie star one day.)

How to spot a dog/creep/wimp.

There are some guys out there who are dogs, some who are creeps and some that are wimps.

Be wary of these men.

Firstly, be wary of the dog. The dog will want nothing more from you than a one-night stand and, once they get what they want, you will never hear from them again. Dogs are the worst. They are users who will do anything and everything to get laid. You need to be on the lookout for these jerks. Never let a guy use you. Unless, of course, you're using him, too. If you're both getting something out of it, fine, that's your business. But if it's just him getting his rocks off, not so fine.

Also, if he's giving off a creep vibe, back away. Well, don't back away, run away. And fast. A dog and a creep have similar characteristics.

How to spot a dog/creep:

- He keeps refilling your wine glass and constantly tells you to "Have more." If he keeps telling you to drink more, he wants in your pants and by getting you liquored up, his chances increase.

- He plays the "I don't kiss on the first date" or the "I'm a virgin" or the "I'm impotent" card. He does this in order to challenge you: "Oh, maybe I will be his first lover" or "Maybe I can break his rule of not kissing" or "I bet I can get that thing going". Don't be fooled! A guy who says these things is usually lying. C'mon, think about it. If they were really impotent, would they tell anyone? No, they wouldn't.

- He's really nice. I mean, really, *really* nice. Too nice. Too interested. Just a hair shy of being creepy.
- He constantly tries to engage you in sex talk. "How many lovers have you had?" Or "What's your favorite position?" Presumably, if he can get you talking and thinking about it, he thinks he can get you into bed.

A guy should be interested in sex but if that's all he talks about with you, that's all he wants from you. He's only out to get laid. Never let him talk you into it and never do anything you don't want to do. I don't care if you ordered the lobster or not. Never do anything you don't want to do.

The bad thing about these creeps is that once you let him know you're not going to have sex with him, he will usually turn into an asshole. And I mean, he will go all Jeckyl and Hyde on you. One minute, he's all over you and the next, he's calling you names. This means he's upset that he's spent a whole twenty dollars on a meal and won't be getting any "payback". If you find yourself out with one of these guys, call a girlfriend or someone else to come and pick you up. *Don't get into a car with him.*

And, never, ever get drunk on a date. Sip your drinks and stop at one. Make it a rule to never get drunk when you're out. Because, once you're drunk, these creeps can and *will* take advantage of you. And, believe me, they will. They get a night of hot sex and you get a bad memory. Not a trade-off I'd like to have.

Also, let's touch on the date-rape drug. There are some creeps out there who will put the drug into your unattended drink. So, never leave your drink unattended when you are out. If you can't avoid it, don't pick it back up. Just ask the bartender for a new one. Keep in mind that it is *always* better safe than sorry.

With any guy that you get a major creep vibe, back away. Always listen to your instinct and never hang around a guy that makes you feel uncomfortable. Just to let you know, there are some guys out there who would like nothing better than to hurt you. Always keep your radar up and, if you feel your spider senses tingling, they're tingling for a reason. Learn to listen to them and never go anywhere with a guy that you don't get a good feeling about. You do not want to get involved with any serial killers or anything, so it is going to be necessary to check him out thoroughly before you proceed. And you want to do it before you invest any time. You can do this by looking him up on the internet. See if anything suspicious comes up. If not, proceed. If so, back off.

Also, you don't want a nut who will hit you either. There might be a reason why he's alone other than the fact that he "hasn't met the right person". That reason might be that he's a nut. You don't want a nut! Again, use your instincts. If at all possible, have a conversation with one of his ex's. If he doesn't have an ex... Well, let's just hope he has at least one.

Be safe! Sure, most men can control themselves pretty good. Most men would rather cut off their hands than hit a woman. However, there are those ones who will hit women. If he ever hits you, hit the door running and never look back. I don't care how "sorry" he was that he did it, or that he "promised" to never do it again. *He will do it again.* And he will play mind games with you to make you stay. And this means, he's a crazy bastard. Run before it's too, late, girl. And don't look back.

Now let's talk about the wimp. If you push him for some reason and he always backs down, he's a wimp. Many men will "take it" for a while just because they don't like conflict. But if he's "taking it" and not asserting himself ever, you might just have a wimp. Wimps are bad news. I know we, as women, love to push men's buttons and we do that to get a reaction. We want to see if he'll stand up for himself. If you do this and he doesn't, he's a wimp and you don't want him. They're usually passive aggressive which can be very emotionally draining. Who needs that?

In a nutshell:

- There are dogs/creeps out there who will get you liquored up and in order to take advantage of you.
- Stop at two drinks.
- If a guy gets belligerent, call someone to come get you. *Don't get into a car with him—ever.* So what if it makes you look like a bitch? Tell him to get over it.
- Feel him out and if you get a creep vibe, don't proceed. You have natural instincts for a reason so if your spider senses start tingling, move away from this guy. He's bad news.
- Why not look him up on the internet? I would.
- Be wary of wimps. You won't respect them and they will drain you emotionally.

Your first date.

He should pick you up and he should pay for everything. If he asks you to go "Dutch" tell him "sure" and that you'll be at the next table. Dining alone.

I always like men who know where they want to take you for a date. That tells me and the rest of the world that he is a confident person. Let him suggest a place and don't say, "I would not be seen dead in there!" Wherever he takes you is fine—unless it's fast-food—but expect him to treat you like a lady.

There may be a slight chance your guy isn't that confident and will want you to suggest a place. This is okay. Suggest a place but don't bankrupt him on the first date. Somewhere nice and quiet where you can converse is good. And get to know him.

On your date you are interviewing this guy to see if he's a potential mate. That's what dates are all about. He's interviewing you, too. I wouldn't ask him everything you want to know about him all at once, but do cover some basics.

Basic things to ask:
- Where do you work? (Good indicator if he's going to be able to take care of you.)
- Have you ever been married? Do you have any kids?
- What are you looking for in a relationship?

Stuff like this should let you know if he's boyfriend or even possibly husband material. But keep it light and easy. Ask him about his favorite movie and what kind of beer he likes and where he went to school.

In order to be safe, I would suggest that you meet the guy at the restaurant or wherever and if you feel comfortable with him, you can let him take you home. This way, if for some reason, you don't feel comfortable being alone with him, or are just overly cautious, it's not a big deal if you leave early. Just tell him you have to work late or whatever and that you'll meet him at the restaurant. You don't have to go into a million different excuses, either. That way, if he turns out to be a slimeball, you can get a quick getaway. "I have a headache" always seems to work.

In a nutshell:

- He should pick you up and pay for dinner.
- The first date should be kept light and easy.

Something to talk about.

When you're out on your date, you might find that the conversation dries up. One way to make sure it doesn't is to always have something to talk about. One way to do that is to always be learning new things.

And, no, you shouldn't look at this as a school assignment. Learning can be fun and now that you're grown up, you—not the teacher—can pick the subject. When you're learning new things or doing new things, you will have so much to talk about. You will always be able to engage others in conversation. All you have to do is open your eyes a little and travel, if possible. Reading the newspaper or watching the news is good, too.

Traveling is great not only because you get to go to cool places but because you get to meet and be around all different kinds of people. Whenever possible, visit a museum and always be on the lookout to expand your horizons in any way possible. Don't just sit around and wait for someone else to come along and ask you to go someplace. Go alone, if necessary. Doing this makes you more confident and more knowledgeable.

Also, always read new books. I find travel books are great reads. Doing all this will not only give you more confidence but it will also help you to be a better conversationalist. And, when you're with a new guy, he'll think you're really smart if you can talk about a number of different things.

In a nutshell:
- Learning new things can give you a lot to talk about on a date.
- Traveling is great.
- Read new books.

Dates over. Now what?

After the date's over, you need to evaluate it. Do you want to see him again? Is this a guy you'd like to know better? Do you have anything in common with him? I mean, there has to be something there that you like. If there is no connection, then don't make a second date. Don't hem-haw about it, either. Just say, "I had a great time but I'm really not ready for a relationship."

Of course, he is going to know what that means. If you have trouble leveling with him after the date, email him. It may seem a little cowardly but it's less messy that way. And be honest about it. Don't make up excuses like you're going out of town or whatever; otherwise, he'll just keep pestering you. Just say that you're not ready for a relationship yet. And, really, you're not. At least not with him.

If you want to see him again, don't sweat it. If he's into you, he'll ask for that second date. If *he* hems-haws about it, then *he* doesn't want to see you again. So thank him for his time and walk away.

Warning: He might do that stupid "waiting for three days to call" game. Don't play it. If he does this, wait three days to call *him* back. This should let him know where you stand. Remember, you're a man magnet and you don't play games. If he asks what took you so long to call back, ask him what took him so long. This lets him know you're onto his game.

One thing, if your date left you feeling "icky", you need to move on. Not much can overcome ick. And by ick I mean creepy, as we discussed before. Find another one if this happens.

In a nutshell:
- After the date, decide if you would like to see him again.
- If you don't want to see him again, tell him so. Or send him an email.
- If you leave the date with a feeling of "ick", then don't see him again. Not much can overcome the feeling of ick.

Always leave him wanting more.

Do you want someone to really, really like you? Then always leave him wanting more. Never give any more of yourself at first than you have to. If you can leave a guy wanting more, he'll want more, believe me. The upside of this? You'll probably never be able to get rid of him. (That may also be the downside, but still...)

A few rules to always leaving him wanting more:
- Never gush.
- Never laugh at a stupid joke. Just chuckle.
- Never show too much interest.

Let's discuss the last rule, "never show too much interest". If you show a guy that you're really interested in him, he'll run with his tail tucked between his legs. I don't know why this is, but men, as I've said a gazillion times, don't want you to like them too much at first. I think it might have something to do with them "proving" their manliness or something like that. Regardless, if you show too much interest, their little minds start racing with nightmare scenarios which can include wedding cakes and baby powder.

If you can always leave them wanting more and show just enough interest to keep them, well, interested, you will have no trouble pulling them into your orbit. If you show him right off the bat that you *really* like him, he's probably not going to really like you. It shows him that he has the power over you and he will not respect you as much. The weird thing about this is that he probably doesn't even realize he's doing this. As you realize, this has no logic to it at all, but that's the way most men play the game of love.

So how do you always leave them wanting more? By playing the part of a man magnet, that's how. Remember, as a man magnet, you don't care that much about this guy. He's cool, you suppose, but he's more than likely not "The One". You're just having a date with him, sharing a drink. Sure, you might be feeling butterflies stir in your stomach but you can't let him know that. You've got him hooked. Just sit back and let him flip around on the line, then reel him in.

This is not a hard thing to do. Just look at it as an assignment, something you have to do in order to "get" him. Keep a little distance and before long, you'll have him eating out of the palm of your hand. Once you know you've hooked him, *then* you let him know how you feel. But always leave him wanting more, even when he knows you're in love.

In a nutshell:
- Always leave him wanting more.
- Never show too much interest right off the bat.

How to know if you've hooked him.

You should be able to tell within a month or so if a guy is falling for you—sometimes you can tell within a few dates. If you have no clue, look for signs.

Signs he's going ga-ga:

- He's always eager to see you and smiles when you come into the room.
- He's calling all the time.
- He's asking for Saturday dates early on in the week.
- He interjects the "love" word into the conversation occasionally: "I love it when you wear your hair like that." Or, "Don't you just love sushi?" Or, "I'd love to take you to dinner again."
- He gives you compliments all the time: "You've got such a hot body." Or, "Wow! Don't you look pretty tonight?"
- He gets a little jealous when other guys check you out. Say for instance, you've heard him say, "Who does that guy think he is?" That means he's jealous. That means, he really likes you. (Of course, not all guys are jealous and some that are *very* jealous can be crazy. Check him out and, if gets too possessive, dump him. If he's too possessive at first, that means he will make you dump all your friends to be with him only.)
- He's mentioned wanting to have kids "someday".
- He sends flowers to your work.

- He's cooked for you and bought you small gifts here and there.

If you're getting some of these signs, the gig is up. It's time to make him into your boyfriend. That is, if you want to make him your boyfriend. Hey, you might be having so much fun, you want to stay single for a while and drive other men as crazy as you've driven this one. It can be addicting. However, this isn't what this part of the book is about. This part is about keeping him once you've got him.

But what if you're not sure he's not going ga-ga? There shouldn't be any doubt but, if you're uncertain, just know that if he's avoiding you in any way, shape or form, he's not falling for you. (Missed dates, no phone calls, etc.) If so, either refer to the later chapter "Suddenly unavailable" or dump him. Remember, you can't make anyone like you. If, for some reason he's not interested in you, then let him go. He's not worth your time and that's because if he's not falling for you, he won't treat you right. And he won't treat you right because he thinks he doesn't have to. He's just not worth it. But most of all, don't fixate on this one guy. If it didn't work out for whatever reason, then it wasn't meant to. Move on, girl.

In a nutshell:
- If he's ga-ga over you, then it's time to get serious.
- If you're not ga-ga over him, break it off ASAP.
- If he's not going ga-ga, move on.

She's a lady.

What you have to keep in mind is that when you first start dating a guy he is "courting you". Yes, that is a very old-fashioned way of looking at it but that's what's going on. In today's world, we women seem to think we don't need to be courted. This might be why we let guys walk all over us. In the "old" days, men had to act like gentlemen or they wouldn't be dating us at all. Now we let them do whatever they damn well please. I say we shouldn't let this happen anymore. Expect to be courted, which is just another way to say "treated well" and you will get treated well. Don't ever be afraid to tell a guy what you expect, whether it's dinner and a movie or that he calls if he's going to be late. If he finds you're not worth the "trouble" then that means *he's* not worth the trouble.

As I keep reiterating, what you have to keep in mind is that you are worth all this. Yes, you are. Any woman deserves to have a guy court her and if he's not willing, then he doesn't deserve the chance at marriage and babies. (I think this is called "natural selection".) If a guy is really into you, he won't be afraid to court you and that means he'll rarely be late or deliberately do anything else to piss you off. And, if he is late or accidentally pisses you off, he'll apologize and have a good excuse. He'll remember your birthday or those little anniversaries. He'll hold the door open for you and he'll be courteous in other ways. In fact, he will be on his best behavior. And why will he do all this? Because he's trying to "get" you and he knows he has to work in order to do so. So, let him work for it. And if he's not willing? Bye-bye, that's what.

But what if he doesn't have money for all of this courting stuff—you ask. What if he doesn't have the time to call because he works long hours? First of all, what's a phone call or a dinner? Nothing, that's what. Secondly, let me tell you a story of a guy I used to date called Bob. Bob and I were in college together and went out for a while. Bob was broke all the time and was working two or three crappy jobs just to get by. Yet, Bob always came up with the cash for dinner and a movie. Bob always held the door open for me and he always showed me a good time, even if he was broke. Bob always called if he was going to be late. And that's because Bob was a good guy. So, if you come across a whiner who doesn't want to do these things to gain your affection, tell him about Bob. If Bob can treat a girl well on his limited resources, so can all these other guys.

You might also want to tell these guys about natural selection and survival of the strongest. What these guys don't realize is that if they're not willing to play the game—or even buy dinner—they don't have a chance of getting their genes into the next generation. And, in the end, that's what all this is about. It's about genetic destiny and the ability to pick the strongest mate for our offspring. Sure, that's very anthropological, but it's true. It's why we do what we do and also why we shouldn't bother with men who can't be bothered to treat us right.

I think the problem is that we women have stopped expecting guys do to their part. A guy can get away with anything now—he can impregnate a woman and run off and he doesn't have to do a damn thing about it. He can forget to call and act like a jerk and put a girl on a booty call list and do all these other things and *we let them*. It's time to put men back in their places, ladies, and all we have to do is to start demanding they treat us like ladies.

For some reason, we have all forgotten that in order for a relationship of any kind to work there has to be give and take. When a guy is courting you, you're "giving" him your time. You're allowing him to see you to see if you're "The One". You're taking your precious time to give him this opportunity. So, therefore, when he's courting you, he is responsible for giving you something in return—flowers, dinners, time, whatever. But he especially needs to give you respect.

We've made it way too easy on men to treat us like crap. Start standing up for yourself and don't be afraid to get treated in the way you like. Believe me, if he can't be bothered to treat you well at this stage of the relationship, he doesn't deserve a chance to be with a girl like you. He deserves to end up alone.

Remember you are worth it. Say it with me: *You are worth it!*

And, yes, I know I keep saying this, but you absolutely *have to* start acting like a woman—a woman who needs a man. Ask him to squash a bug or pick up something heavy for you. He has to show you he's a man and if he feels emasculated around you, he's never going to want to be with you. However, don't ever take his crap. If he screws up, let him know and make him pay for screwing up. If you let him get away with it, he'll *always* get away with it.

If he forgets your birthday or does something else to piss you off, tell him about it. Don't yell or scream, just give him a simple, "I thought you were better than that." This will make him clean up his act real quick.

Any relationship has a power struggle. Give him the power over some things, or at least let him think he has it, and retain power in other things. Let him take you over in the bedroom but never let him walk all over you.

The thing about men is that they rarely, if ever, change. Good thing: What you see is usually what you get. Bad thing: Sometimes you don't like what you see.

In a nutshell:
- Never let a guy walk all over you.
- Demand respect and you will get it.

Let's talk about sex.

Sex confuses a lot of people. When do you give it up? Will he think you're a ho-bag if you want it on the second date? We put so much into it it's a wonder we get anything out of it in the first place.

As far as sex goes, men are weird about it. It's men, not women, who have made up these stupid rules. So now everyone has to suffer. It's no wonder we're all so miserable.

It's like this crazy Catch-22. If you give it up too soon, he'll lose interest. If you wait too long, he'll go somewhere else. You have to give it up at the exact right moment otherwise your relationship will be tainted from then on. You have to wait for the "perfect" moment or he'll think you're some kind of slut. Not that it matters that *he's* the one who wants to do it with *you*. Men have this terrible double standard when it comes to sex. If you give it to him too "soon", he's probably going to think that you're giving it to everyone else a little *too* soon. And that you've given it away quite a lot.

Without sounding old-fashioned, I do think there was a reason that women during the "good old days" didn't have sex until they were married. Don't start rolling your eyes yet, just listen. If a man is so attracted to a woman that he'll wait until he marries her, there is no doubt that she's "The One" and that means he will treat her right.

This is the attitude you need to acquire. No, I am not saying to wait until you get married to have sex. But don't give it out like you would Halloween candy. Why? Because if you make him wait, he'll appreciate it even more. He'll think you're special. And what are a few dates anyway? Nothing. If he's not willing to wait that long on you, he needs to hire an escort and get it over with.

You are a precious commodity. You are what he wants. Make him work for it. Think of it this way: If something happens, is it him that's going to carry a baby in his belly? No. Take all this into consideration when weighing the pros and cons of when to give it up. There are risks involved, you know?

As I said in an earlier chapter, most men do not like overtly sexual women. Why? Because it's too easy! They think, "Why does she want to give it up so soon? There must be something wrong with her." Yeah, she's horny, that's what's wrong.

Still, it's sad fact of life, but it's true. Men have really taken this too far. My suggestion is to give it up when *you* want to give it up. Don't play games with any guy. We all know that sex is one of life's greatest joys. Believe me, this one's your call and there's not a damn thing he can do about it.

So what to do? Wait him out, that's what you do. If this means you give him blue-balls, then that's what it means. Besides, it was men who came up with this double standard crap to begin with. It's time we beat them at this little game. After all, we've got what they want most.

If you're confused and don't know what to do, try this: To begin with, on the first date, just allow him to kiss your cheek. That's it. Some guys are weird when it comes to this stuff and they're not weird because they're *weird*, but they're weird because this is what they've been taught. All their lives, people have told them that girls are chaste and any girl worth having won't give it up too soon. So, make him work for it.

A suggested timetable:
- First date: A kiss on the cheek.
- Second date: A kiss on the mouth, but no tongue.
- Third date: Give him a gut-wrenching kiss that will make his knees buckle.
- Fourth date: Give him sex *only* if you're comfortable with it.
- Fifth date: By this time, you should know if you're going to have sex but you can still wait more if you like. That is, if you're really into torturing a guy. But hey, if that's what you want to do, do it.
- Something else to consider: Only have sex when *you* feel comfortable. If that means making him wait six months, then so be it.

The point is to always, *always* leave a guy wanting more. That is the biggest secret of being a man magnet. If you can leave him wanting more, then you'll never get rid of him. Seriously, try it and see. This will drive him crazy.

When and if you have sex, the most important thing you can do is overcome your inhibitions. You want to drive a man crazy in bed. You want him to think that he can't get what you've got anywhere but with you. There is a big secret to being good in bed. Wanna know what it is? GET INTO IT! Let him know how good it feels when he's doing stuff to you. Never give him the "cold fish" treatment and that means, never just lie there and act like a...well, a cold fish.

But, more importantly, don't be afraid to do stuff to him. That means allow your inhibitions to ride. Get the most you can get out of it, and give him the most you can. Sex is great when both parties are equally into it. If you're naturally shy in bed, learn to overcome inhibitions by reading erotica, sex books or watching "dirty" movies. And, of course, you should have a vibrator to "practice" with. If you can't give yourself an orgasm in that way, he probably won't be able to either. No, this won't turn you into a slut, but it will allow you to see that sex isn't that big of a deal and it'll also allow you to get the most out of it as well. If you're not getting anything out of it, then why bother at all?

One last thing. This should go without saying, but you need to be aware that there are risks involved with sex such as pregnancy and diseases. Educate yourself and always be doubly careful. Condoms, as well as an alterative birth control method such as the pill, are a must.

In a nutshell:

- Men are weird about sex.
- Give it up when and only when you feel comfortable. If you're not sure, check out the suggested timetable.
- When you do give it to him, really relax and get into it. He'll be begging for more, believe me.
- Be aware of risks of sex—pregnancy and STDs.

Suddenly unavailable.

Let's say for some reason your new guy is starting to act a little... Well, he's acting weird. He's not calling when he says he'll call or he's canceled a few dates. What can a girl do? This is easy. Ask yourself if this guy is worth it.

Men are easy to understand. No, I take that back. Men who have huge egos or commitment issues aren't easy. The rest of them are actually pretty easy to figure out. And if you can figure out how to work men, like I've been saying all along, you aren't going to have any trouble keeping one. So, if you find your new guy is pulling away, you've apparently got a hold of one of those commitment-phobic guys. Ooh, he's so scared you'll want to get married someday. If this is the case, he's not worth your trouble, lady.

If, however, you really like him and want to give it one more shot, do this: Start pulling away. That's right, reverse it on him. If he takes this clue and breaks up with you, then why did you want him in the first place? He was never going to make you happy.

That's right. Pull back a little. Just a touch. Not enough to make him think you're losing interest, but enough to let him know he's not the only fish in the sea.

You do this by becoming *suddenly unavailable.* I know it's hard because you probably really like this guy. You don't want him to think you don't like him. You don't want him to get any ideas. Well, okay, don't do it and keep being his doormat. But, look at it like this: If you start chasing after him and he breaks up with you anyway, he wasn't falling for you in the first place and you've just saved yourself a lot of torment and heartbreak.

If you spend every waking hour with any guy, you're asking for trouble. It will kill even the best relationship. You never give him any space to think about you or to miss you. If you're constantly in his face, he's going to think, "She's crowding me and it won't be long until she wants to know why I haven't asked her to marry me. I better nip this in the bud."

On the other hand, if *you* pull back a little, he's going to think, "I really like her. Why didn't she return my calls? Is she seeing someone else?"

This will drive him crazy. This will put you in the forefront of his mind. He will start thinking of you all the time.

So how do you do it? It's easy. Don't return a call every once in a while. When he asks to see you, occasionally tell him, "Oh, I've got something planned for that night. Let's do it next week." "Forget" to meet him a time or two and when he asks what happened say. "Oh, no, did I do that? I'm sorry. I must have forgotten!" If you see him out somewhere, like at the mall or wherever, make sure he sees you, but then don't let him know you saw him. Fall into the crowd and when he asks about it later say, "I didn't see you. Sorry."

Believe me, this will let you know whether or not he's planning on sticking around. You want to see if this guy is biting? Start pulling away and you'll be able to tell. You want to drive him crazy? Become suddenly unavailable and you will. It's all about never appearing too eager. It's all about being "unavailable" to your new guy and once you are, he'll realize how much he wants you.

As I've said, men are easy and they normally want what they can't have. If they can't have you, they will die trying to get you. Of course there are exceptions to this rule, as with anything, but for most "normal" guys, it should work like a charm. And, I say, if he's already pulling back, what could it hurt if you do the same? You're just beating him to the punch.

Do keep in mind that you're taking a gamble, girl. He might go for it and he might not. Either way, you'll find out if you have a future together.

In a nutshell:

- If you find your guy is acting weird and not returning calls, slowly pull away and don't return his calls a few times.
- This is called becoming "suddenly unavailable".
- This will let you know whether he plans on sticking around or not. If he doesn't after you do it, you've just saved yourself a bundle of heartbreak.
- Also, only do this if your guy is acting weird.

The #1 rule to keeping a man once you've sealed the deal.

Again, feminists will eat me alive for saying this, but here goes nothing. The number one rule to keeping a man is this: Do not let yourself go once you've sealed the deal.

In essence:
- Don't gain a bunch of weight.
- Always dress nicely when you see him.
- If you see another guy checking you out, smile and say, "I think that guy's checking me out. How funny." Then turn back to him and give him a kiss on the cheek. (This lets him know he's got himself a hottie.)

A few other things to keep in mind:
- Don't emasculate him and by this I mean, don't treat him like he's less than a man. He has balls for a reason. Never tell him what to do or snap your fingers at him. And please, don't ever ask him to hold your purse while you're shopping. Always, always treat him like a man. If you give respect like this, you will be respected in turn.
- Never insult his mother. No matter what she does, try to keep your calm. You can insult her after you get married.

Besides that, there are a few other things you can do to "keep" him. One of the biggest things is: If he wants to spend time with his friends, let him. If there's a chance he's going to fall out of love with you within the space of a few hours, then it wasn't meant to be. Some girls are very insecure when it comes to this stuff. Don't be one of those insecure girls or you might have to start hunting another man.

It's easy to make your man's life miserable when he does something you don't like, such as seeing his loser friends. You can also threaten him and all this other stuff to keep him "in line". But why would you want to? Don't do it. If he wants you, he will come back to you and if not, you're better off alone. Who knows what he and his loser friends are doing? Who cares? If the worst thing he does is go to a stripclub, and it drives you crazy, you need to get a grip. Believe it or not, there are far worse things he could be doing. Remember, if he's coming home to you, he still loves you and not the stripper who took all of his money.

If you don't make a big deal out of things like this, then he'll wonder how he got so lucky. Believe me, he will. Of course, this doesn't mean being his doormat. This doesn't mean taking his crap. Always stand up to him and if he does something you don't like, let him know about it. But don't make him pay for days over it. A few hours should do it.

Instead of fuming that he's going out with his friends, go out with yours. When he asks what you did, just tell him, "Me and the girls went out for a few drinks. What did you do?"

Be cool and he'll think you're cool.

Always take some time for yourself. I know when you fall in love you want to spend every waking moment with your new honey, but do that and prepare for relationship death. Keep seeing your girlfriends, don't overlook your hobbies and do the things you loved to do before you fell in love.

But most importantly, do things for him that make him happy and make your time together special.

Some things to do that will make him get real happy:

- Cook him dinner. Nothing fancy. Man food is best. The pot roast and potatoes kind of meal or fried chicken—most men *love* fried chicken. This is what he likes. Give it to him.

- Get into sex. Maybe even suggest ways you can do it "differently" from time to time. (If you don't know "how", read sex books and erotica, like I suggested earlier.)

- Men aren't like women. Most of them won't cry if you forget their birthday. But be one of those girls who don't forget. Make a big deal out of his birthday, just like you expect him to make a big deal out of yours.

- Plan a few out of town trips.

- Dress up as a nurse or a school girl and surprise him. Wow. You've just written your own ticket.

This lets him know that you think he's so special that you'd go to all this trouble. And that's the exact kind of reaction you want.

In a nutshell:

- If he wants to go out with his buddies, let him do it and don't throw a screaming fit.

- Continue to do the things you love even if you are in a heavy-duty relationship.

- Do special things for him from time to time.

He's un-trainable if...

When a woman gets into a relationship with a man, she understands that if the relationship is going to continue, she's going to have to bring her new guy up to speed about her standards and what she expects out of a boyfriend. Like being able to depend on a guy to show up on time or to send a flower every once in a while. Not all men are hip to this. If your man is like this, then you may have to do a little pushing and bitching to get what you want. This also lets him know what you expect out of the relationship. A little pushing and bitching isn't necessarily a bad thing because it lets him know you won't settle for second best. And most men are trainable whether they know they are or not.

However, some men, no matter what you do, are un-trainable. And by being un-trainable, I mean, no matter what you do he won't bend or improve. For example, if you ask him to be on time and he always shows up late. Or if you ask for a foot rub, he snarls his nose. These men aren't worth keeping around simply because if you tie the knot, they'll always want to know why you need so many shoes and why you cry when they forget your birthday.

He's un-trainable if:
- He spends all his money on wine, women and song.
- He spends all of his time with his buddies.
- He never takes you anywhere.
- He never asks how your day was.
- He acts like he doesn't give a crap about you.

- He still lives at home with mom and dad. (If he's cute and you really like him, you can make an exception and go out with him a few times and perhaps, try to persuade him to get his own place. If he doesn't within a few months, he's not going to and you're wasting your time.)
- He does anything and everything in his power to "get you into bed" without actually trying to do something nice for you.
- He asks you to pay for dinner.
- He asks to borrow money.
- He asks you to see if your roommate likes him.
- He's a wimp. (Which means he will be easy to train but hard to get rid of, if need be.)
- He gives off a loser or creep vibe at any time. That might just be his "real" self coming through.

In a nutshell:

- Some men are un-trainable.
- If so, ditch 'em.

The bastard broke up with me! (Or, I just had to break up with the bastard.)

Keep in mind that this might be a possibility. And if he does break up with you, go find yourself a new one. You're a man magnet after all. You can get just about any guy you want. Besides that, you know it was fun while it lasted. You did enjoy yourself, didn't you? At least a little bit? And the next time, you'll enjoy yourself even more.

Heartbreak is a bitch but keep in mind that you won't be lonely long. I know it's hard, but just get through it. Read a favorite book and cry your heart out. After you've done this for a few days, wipe your tears and get dressed cause you're going out. There are many guys who'd love a girl like you and all you have to do is show up and let them know you're available. Get right back out there and get busy.

On the other hand, what if you decide you don't want to date this guy anymore? Break it off before he really falls in love with you. You need to know that once a guy falls in love, *he's in love.* There's not much anyone can do about it, either. So, decide after the first few dates if you like him enough to warrant this reaction. If not, it might be time to pull the plug.

Breaking up is hard to do and it never gets any easier over time. In fact, the longer you wait, the harder it is. Some women wait so long, they find themselves married to the guy they wanted to dump. (Extreme, I know, but it has happened, believe it or not.) Don't be one of these women!

Do it before it goes too far, otherwise you might end up marrying this jerk and hating him for the rest of your life. Not a situation any woman wants to find herself in.

And don't play games like not returning his call. The next time he calls, just tell him it's been fun but you need some time alone. Be honest. It will hurt him, you have to know, but doing it quickly and to the point gets it over and with as little pain as possible.

Don't do anything unless you want to do it. You don't have to make any excuses for it, either. I mean, if you stay with him because you feel sorry for him or you're afraid of hurting his feelings, what good is that going to do either of you? If you want to get rid of him, get rid of him. Dump him like yesterday's news. How to do it with as little pain as possible? Call him up and say, "Listen, Earl, it's been nice but I really can't see you anymore. I want to break up." Or, "This just isn't working for me and it's probably not working for you. So, let's call it quits, okay?" Or, you can make up your own excuse using more or less tact, but never tell a guy that you can still be "friends". That's insulting to humans in general and we all know it's a big fat lie.

So, don't pussy-foot around. Get right to the point and get it done. If he freaks out on you, tell him you're sorry and hang up the phone. You don't have time to listen to his whining. You've got more men to torture.

In a nutshell:
- Heartbreak is a bitch. But you can and will get through it in order to get to the next guy who'll be so much better for you.
- If you want to do the dumping, do it ASAP. Don't lead a guy on and don't stay with one because you feel bad about wanting to break it off.

In conclusion.

I know this was a lot of stuff to consume, so just take it in increments if you need to or just use the parts of it that apply to you. Do what you have to do in order to get yourself out there and find a good man. It really doesn't take that much. You've got everything you need. Just using your assets from time to time and acting like woman is all it takes.

In the end, it's up to you. It's up to you to get yourself a man magnet outfit and to build your confidence. It's up to you to attract that man who's going to bring joy and love into your life. And, yes, he's out there somewhere. He's waiting for you just as you're waiting for him. Just think, he wants someone like you just as bad as you want someone like him. Doesn't it make the butterflies in your stomach stir just thinking about it?

Ah, hell, I am a hopeless romantic. Get out there and get to it, girl.

Printed in the United States
67963LVS00005B/51